THE MANDAL COMMISSION AND MANDALISATION: A CRITIQUE

THE MANDAL COMMISSION AND MANDALISATION : A CRITIQUE

SHRIRAM MAHESHWARI
Professor of Political Science and Public Administration
Indian Institute of Public Administration
NEW DELHI

CONCEPT PUBLISHING COMPANY, NEW DELHI 110059

ISBN 8-7022-338-5

First Published 1991

Published and Printed by
Ashok Kumar Mittal
Concept Publishing Company
A/15-16, Commercial Block, Mohan Garden
NEW DELHI 110059 (India)

Lasertypeset by
Microtech Advance Printing Systems (Pvt.) Ltd.
H-13, Bali Nagar
NEW DELHI 110015

To

Students

Who are presently making sacrifices

for the Integrated Future of Mother India

Preface

The year 1990 has been truly the year of B.P. Mandal, the Chairman of the Second Backward Classes Commission which the first Janata Government, remaining in office during 1977-79, had appointed. This Commission was form 1 on 20 December 1978, more than a year of the coming into power of the Janata Party, and it submitted its report on 31 December 1980. For nearly ten years, the Mandal Commission Report remained unattended, with little notice taken of it. It does find a mention in the National Front's election manifesto (1989) but no one apparently cared to read the report, much less take it seriously. Even the manifesto drafters apparently did not know its full nomenclature: it was referred to merely as 'Mandal Commission'. Also, reservation for backward castes was neither a commonly discussed subject during the election speeches of V.P. Singh and other front-ranking leaders of the Janata Party.

The Mandal Commission Report is a casually and hastily prepared document which is replete with errors of all kinds. In order to give to itself a veneer of rationality and objectivity, the Mandal Commission sought to impart to its report a research base, but even a superficial reading would disprove the claim. The caste-data used by the Mandal Commission are based on the census report of 1931. Since then, nothing short of a qualitative change has occurred in the Indian scenario, but Mandal takes no account of it. Social mobility has itself brought about tremendous change: so has the country's partition. What about the impact of democracy and development? But the Mandal Commission shows its utter innocense about them. A report based on such fallible premises loses its reliability for policy-making. Equally, the ethical standard shown by the Commission is questionable.

Yet, the Report was, suddenly, retrieved from the shelves. Apparently without caring to study it seriously, its acceptance was announced in the Parliament. The policy underlying the Mandal recommendations is apt to be of deep and far-reaching consequence to almost every family in the country but the report was not nationally debated to develop a consensus. As a rule, a major policy matter like job reservation of this range and magnitude is discussed within the cereer bureaucracy. But bureaucracy too was by-passed. The decision, in other words, was wholly political. Though the supporting parties of the minority National Front used to be consulted on various matters before governmental decisions were taken but on the question of job reservation no discussion or consultation occurred. The decision on the Mandal Report was thus unilateral: the Report was not discussed even within the party forums.

The Mandal is now the Law of the Land

The present work is focused on the Mandal Commission, its Report, the governmental decisions and the social and political implications flowing from them. To impart a historical perspective, the first Kaka Kalelkar Backward Classes Commission (1953-55) is freely referred to. Parts of the material used in the book were previously published in the form of two articles in *The Statesman* and *The Hindu* respectively. The author is grateful to them for the permission accorded to use these pieces in the present work.

It is hoped, the work will contribute to educate the general public on a facet of social life carrying profound meaning for the country's future.

Navagraha
19 September 1990
156 Golf Links
NEW DELHI

S R M

Contents

CHAPTER ONE

The Concept of Reservation and the Constitution

Public Services constitute the instrument available to a modern government for carrying out its multifarious responsibilities — regulatory, developmental, promotional and otherwise. Both the efficiency and sufficiency of the government are determined by the professional competence of the personnel employed in it. Indeed, no government can expect to travel much beyond what its public services permit it to do. Therefore, the public services are of critical importance to the government, being its most valuable asset. It is this realisation which has induced all modern governments to recruit in their services persons who possess the highest level of professional competence. This implies acceptance of merit as the basis of public recruitment. Historically, the criterion of public recruitment was patronage and it is only in the later part of the nineteenth century that merit as proven through a competitive examination gradually replaced it in various countries. Thanks to the celebrated Macaulay Report on the Indian Civil Service, reporting in 1854, merit was adopted as the established basis of public recruitment in India, 'Hitherto the admissions (to the Indian Civil Service) have been given by favour. They are hence-forward to be gained by superiority in an intellectual competition'. According to the Committee, the intellectual test was also the best moral test; 'early superiority in science and literature generally indicates the existence of some qualities which are securities against vice-industry, self-denial, a taste for pleasures not sensual, a laudable desire of honourable distinction, a still more laudable desire to obtain the approbation of friends and relations'. The first open competitive examination was held in 1855 to recruit persons to the Indian Civil Service; and since then the public services in India began to be based on merit. There was a set back to it when under the plan of

Indianisation of the public services consequent upon the submission of the Report of the Lee Commission on the Superior Civil Services in India (1922-24), the British rulers began to appoint persons belonging to different communities in the land. This was part of the colonial policy of divide and rule with a view of perpetrating foreign dominion over India. But the secular forces always upheld merit being retained as the base of public recruitment, the only exception made was for what were then called the 'Depressed Castes'.

The welfare oriented action was part of the larger social animations permeating the national freedom movement. When India won its Independence in 1947 and set down to draft its Constitution the social concerns were very loud and vivid. The environment was also not unsupportive. Rather, almost everywhere, the modern State found itself engaged in developing for itself an interventionist role of social engineering. One instance of such a broadening role is in the form of earmarking of a certain percentage of jobs in public institutions for the disadvantaged groups of the population. This policy is known by various names – reservation system, quota system, affirmative action, positive discrimination, reverse discrimination, etc. To avoid possible confusion one should first come to terms with the term.

Discrimination is defined as different and selective application (or disregard) of rights, laws or organisational policies to potential or actual employees.[1] This is the base to which all such terms seek integration. Reverse discrimination is 'preferential treatment of individuals or groups who had previously been discriminated against because of their race, national origin, sex, age, religion or handicap, to the exclusion of other individuals or groups'.[2] In other words, it is discrimination in favour of members of certain groups in order to rectify an inherent inequality of opportunity experienced by those groups. Its overall goal is to incorporate the socially and economically disadvantaged groups into the mainstream of political, social and economic institutions. Major fields of discrimination are employment, education, housing, etc. Protective discrimination is an attempt more or less to equalise inequalities in society, and thus in its broad secular sense it rejects the Darwinian ideology believing as it does in State intervention to bring the disadvantaged sections in society more or less on a par with the rest. It is thus a rectificatory device to curb and correct the interplay of free market forces.

Birth-based Categories

In India, society, that is, Hindu society finds itself stratified permanently, so to say. The caste has rigidly divided the Hindus into various birth-based categories, some advantageously placed and some disadvantageously. Once born in a caste, one has to remain confined to that caste, and the incumbent inherits all the perks and disabilities *ex officio*. The 'sudras', destined to live on the fringe of society, and the 'untouchables', those outside the four-fold classification condemned to live on the fringe of the fringe, suffer from numerous stigmas, social and economic, which are ascribable to birth itself.

Confronting such a spectacle, the State in India has been obliged by the Constitution to earmark for the disadvantaged a certain percentage of seats in the legislative bodies at all levels as well as of posts in the country's public services. Admission to institutions of specialised education also provides for reservation for such groups. The two sections, identified by the Constitution of India for such preferential treatment are the scheduled castes and the scheduled tribes.

Reservation is vast in its scope covering as it does large areas of public life at all the levels of government. Under reservation fall subjècts such as reservation of seats in the elective democratic bodies like Parliament and State Legislatures and in educational institutions including scientific and technical institutions. It certainly includes reservation system in the country's public services. The present work has a restrictive coverage: it discusses the public policy of job reservation in the public service under the Government of India with special reference to the Mandal Report on reservation for the backward castes, and then goes on to examine the implementation, emerging trends as well as implications of such a policy. Finally, it makes a few policy recommentations.

As said earlier, Indian society is not a socially homogeneous one, and a powerful cause of inequality is the caste system itself among the Hindus. Certain castes have historically been ascribed the bottom place and have remained backward, socially, economically, educationally, culturally and otherwise. It is then argued, they stand in need of a set of concessions *vis-a-vis* the other more advantageously placed castes so that they could come on a par with the latter and get a fair share in the country's public services as in other walks of life. The Constitution of India, while guaranteeing 'equality of opportunity' to all in matters of public employment, enjoins on the State to reserve in the public services under it appointments or posts in favour of any 'backward class of citizens'.[3] The Constitution does not itself define the term 'backward', but B.R. Ambedkar, the Chairman of the Constitution Drafting Committee, interpreted it to mean 'scheduled castes'[4] and 'scheduled tribes'.[5] Article 335 of the Constitution enjoins on both the Central and State Governments, the responsibility of making provision for appointment for the scheduled castes and scheduled tribes, in the public services consistent, of course, with the maintenance of efficiency in the administration. The government has made detailed rules under such a constitutional provision and, accordingly, the percentage of reservation for the scheduled castes at present stands at 15 per cent and for the scheduled tribes at 7.5 per cent, the underlying principle being their proportion to the population. In all, thus, 22.5 per cent of government jobs are reserved for members belonging to these castes and tribes. Similarly, members of these two groups get age concession also: the upper age limit in their case has been raised by five years: this is purported to neutralise the disadvantages of late start in life. As a result, more and more candidates belonging to these castes and tribes have begun to enter the public services. This is confirmed in Tables 1.1 and 1.2:

TABLE 1.1: Representational increase of the scheduled castes

Group of Service	Scheduled Castes			Percentage in 1989
	in 1965	in 1987	in 1989	
A	328	4752	5204	6.51
B	564	7857	10021	11.65
C	96114	308119	330330	14.85
D	201273	234743	223045	20.41

TABLE 1.2: Representational increase of the scheduled tribes

Group of Service	Scheduled Tribes			Percentage in 1989
	in 1965	in 1987	in 1989	
A	52	1182	1373	2.24
B	103	1450	1720	2.00
C	12390	90160	100425	4.52
D	38444	68220	70583	6.46

Though the representation of the scheduled castes and schedule tribes in Group A posts is 6.51 per cent and 2.24 per cent respectively in 1989, their representation in the IAS is far better. In the IAS, the representation of the secheduled castes is more than nine per cent and of the scheduled tribes more than five per cent. Also, a considerable increase has been resigtered in the representation of these communities both in terms of absolute numbers and in their percentage to the total number of employees in all the four clusters of the Central Government. This can be seen from Table 1.3.

TABLE 1.3: Reservation of the scheduled castes and scheduled tribes in Services in 1987

Sl. No.	Group	Total Employees	Scheduled Castes	Percentage	Scheduled Tribes	Percentage
1	2	3	4	5	6	7
1.	A	57707	4752	18.23	1182	2.05
2.	B	75483	7857	10.41	1450	1.92
3.	C	2131666	308119	14.45	90160	4.23
4.	D	1168312	234143	20.09	68220	5.84
	Total:	3433168	554871	16.18	161012	4.69

Of late, the government has started getting the scheduled caste candidates even for posts requiring upto middle-level technical qualifications. This shows that the reservation policy in operation since 1950 (indeed since 1943 for the scheduled castes though in a limited way) has begun to produce results. However, men far out number women among the successful scheduled caste members, which is but to be expected even though it is not desirable. Though no correct information on it is presently available, an intelligent guess is that nearly 60 per cent of the new scheduled caste entrants into the public services are the 'second generation' beneficiaries (being sons and daughters of already beneficiary parents). The remaining 40 per cent of them owe their success to education.

Goals of Social Justice not Served

This has a lesson for the national policy-makers. The second-generation beneficiaries do not suffer from social and educational handicaps characteristic of their parents and thus need not get into the public services through lowered recruitment standards. They are elitist in their origin and upbringing, and to confer concessions on them in the matter of recruitment is not contributive to the goals of social justice especially in the context of a vast army of unemployed youth. A need for de-schedulising such 'repeat' groups among these communities appears, therefore, to be fair. Also, expansion of educational facilities for the members of the scheduled castes and scheduled tribes appears to be the most effective way for giving them parity with the rest in the society in regard to recruitment to the public services. Arrangement of pre-civil service entry coaching may be much more effective, at least in the long run.

One should also not overlook an uneven spread of benefits reaped by members of the scheduled castes and scheduled tribes. The communities clubbed under the scheduled castes are themselves not internally homogeneous, some being far less backward than others. Consequently the fruits of reservation are getting increasingly cornered by the more forward castes among the scheduled castes, thus keeping the really downtrodden where they virtually were in the past.

The policy of reservation in the matter of public recruitment has since 1975 been extended to the field of promotion also. Promotion may be defined as recruitment from within, and as such it is a demoralising personnel practice to base it (promotion) on any creterion other than that of seniority or merit. There are as a result instances of senior officers turning junior to their scheduled caste colleagues in a matter of a few years.

Until the advent of the National Front Government (V.P. Singh), reservation in an organised form was applicable only to these two categories – scheduled castes and scheduled tribes. Surely, it has existed for the physically handicapped and the ex-servicemen also but these disadvantaged groups enjoyed, no such concessions for the higher civil service — Groups A and B.

NOTES

1. Ivan S. Banki: *Dictionary of Administration and Management*, Los Angeles, Systems Research Institute, 1981, p. 267.
2. *Ibid.*, p. 600.
3. Article 16-4.

4. Untouchables or depressed castes among the Hindus, enumerated in a schedule prepared by the government. Hence the term 'scheduled castes'.
5. Earlier known as primitive or aboriginal tribes these are included in an official schedule. Hence the term 'scheduled tribes'.
6. India, Ministry of Personnel, Public Grievances and Pensions: *Annual Report, 1987-88*, p. 12.

CHAPTER TWO

Move Towards Mandalisation

Reservation of jobs in the country's public services for what are called backward classes has acquired top-level national importance in view of the National Front Government's recent decision (7 August 1990) to reserve 27 per cent of posts for 'other backward classes' under the Central Government and public undertakings. Earlier, in its Election Manifesto of 1989, the National Front publicly supported 'substantial reservations in employment, education and public offices to backward classes' observing at the same time that 'the recommendations of the Mandal (Backward Classes) Commission will be implemented expeditiously'.[1] while delivering his address to the joint session of both the Houses of Parliament on 20 December 1989, the President of India, R. Venkataraman, observed:

> 'The scheduled castes and scheduled tribes continue to be victims of social and economic injustice. The government's primary aim will be to ensure economic and social justice to them so that they can lead their lives with dignity and honour. The reservation for the scheduled castes and scheduled tribes in the legislatures will be extended by a further period of ten years. The government will take appropriate steps to implement the recommendations of the Mandal Commission'.[2]

Constitutional Background

The Constitution of India is loudly solicitous about the welfare of the backward classes of the Indian society; and while expressly providing for the reservation of posts in the country's public administration for two of such classes, namely, the scheduled castes and scheduled tribes, it makes a general mention of similar promotional measures for what it calls 'other backward classes' (OBCs). Job reservation for the scheduled castes and scheduled tribes is a specific constitutional obligation on the part of the State but it is not exactly so for the 'other backward classes'. Historically, the Government of India has set aside, ever since the inception of the present Constitution, positions only for the scheduled castes and scheduled tribes. Extension of these benefits to 'other backward classes' did not win the Centre's approval until the recent 'momentous' decision by the National Front Government. What the Constitution says about the OBCs is about the State's obligation to set up a Commission to investigate the conditions of socially and educationally backward classes and the difficulties under which they labour and to make recommendations as to the steps that should be taken to remove such difficulties and to improve their condition. To give the necessary publicity, the Commission's Report is to be presented to the President of India which would be laid, along with a memorandum explaining the executive action, before Parliament. Two Backward Class Commissions have been set up since the enforcement of the Constitution – one under Kaka Kalelkar in 1953 and the other under Bindhyeshri Prasad Mandal in 1978 (reporting respectively in 1955 and 1980).

The Kaka Kalelkar Commission

The Kaka Kalelkar Commission had a broad-based membership. It included members even from non-backward communities, which injected a wider perspective to it within which it viewed the problem. As the Constitution wanted the amelioration measures for these communities to be consistent with the need for administrative efficiency, the Commission failed to produce an unanimous report: five out of 11 members of the Commission submitted separate notes of dissent. The Commission, in its majority report, recommended a system of reservation of posts in the country's civil service: it was to be 25 per cent in Class I (or Group A), 33.33 per cent in Class II and 40 per cent in Classes III and IV, urging at the same time that the best candidates should, as a rule, be recruited by means of a competitive examination without any regard to caste considerations. In his forwarding letter, Kaka Kalelkar, the Chairman, set his face firmly and resolutely against caste being made the basis of reservation in public services. He emphatically wrote:

> 'I am definitely against reservation in government services for any community for the simple reason that the services are not meant for the servants but they are meant for the service of society as a whole.'

Kaka Kalelkar recognised the central role of public administration in the society and favoured recruitment of only the best men available in the land. He ridiculed the practice of reservation by categorically declaring: 'Reservation of posts for certain backward communities would be as strange as reservation of patients for particular doctors. The patients are not meant to supply adequate or proportionate clientele to all the doctors, whatever their qualifications.' He recommended the principle of 'no reservation' but 'generous preference'. His firm view was that backwardness in society could be tackled on a basis other than that of caste. Kaka Kalelkar's views are reproduced in Chapter Six.

The Kalelkar Commission, (its recommendations being reproduced in Chapter Seven), failed to formulate any objective criteria for identifying 'backward classes', which made the Government of India reject its recommendations. The Commission had classified a very large section of the population as backward, and if special assistance had to be given to such large numbers, the Government argued, the 'really needy will be swapped by the multitude'. The government preferred economic criterion for the definition of 'backward class'.

The Mandal Commission

The Second Backward Classes Commission was set up in 1978 by the Janata Government, its chairman being B.P. Mandal. The Commission had five members, all but one drawn from the backward castes and the remaining one from the scheduled castes. Unlike the composition of the first Backward Classes Commission which was broad-based, the second Commission had a membership which was exclusively from the backward castes. This partisanship reflected itself in its untampered redicalism. As against 2,399 backward classes identified by the first Commission the Mandal Commission spread itself much more widely, listing no fewer than 3,743 castes as backward. It is to be noted that between 1953 and 1978, the number of backward castes should have shown a decline to reflect the impact, however marginal, of the successive programmes of development. The Mandal Commission was apparently unmindful of such inconsistencies. At its hand, the population of other backward classes bacame impressive. It boldly concluded that 52 per cent of the country's population comprised backward castes. The Mandal Commission accordingly agrued that 52 per cent of all posts under the Central Goverenment ought to be reserved for the backward castes. As the recommendation of 52 per cent could go against the earlier judgment of the Supreme Court of India which had laid down that reservation of posts must be below 50 per cent, the Commission proposed reservation to be pegged at a figure which, when added to 22.5 per cent for the scheduled castes and scheduled tribes, remains below 50 per cent. 'In view of this legal constraint the Commission is obliged to recommend a reservation of 27 per cent only, even though their population is almost twice this figure.' The Mandal recommendations are reproduced in Chapter Eight.

A word about the composition of the Backward Classes Commission appears to be called for. A Commission of Inquiry is normally appointed when a certain issue has acquired wide public importance and the State seeks the considered advice of persons who already possess a level of subject-matter competence and are expected to go deep into the problem and come out with their considered recommendations. In short, a commission acquires the colour and character of an adjudicatory organ, which is expected to examine the issues deeply and impartially and then come out with its recommendations. The government appointed B.P. Mandal as Chairman of the Backward Classes Commission. But he was a politician and himself belonged to a backward caste. That he was fabulously wealthy is also true and well-known. In addition to him, the Commission had four members not many of whom possessed judicial experience and all came from the disadvantaged castes. This kind of composition violates the first and foremost norm of an inquiry, namely, the principle of objectivity. The one-sided membership of the Mandal Commission produced a Report which became one-sided, being little more than the lobbyists' report. The Mandal Commission lacked a wider perspective and did not sufficiently take into account the larger issues such as the need for an efficient and professional civil service capable of undertaking growingly complex tasks of democracy and development.

One should also note that the need to identify the better-off among backward classes to prevent them from cornering all the benefits of reservation has been highlighted in a note of dissent to the Mandal

Commission report. A member of the Commission, L.R. Naik, an ex-MP and a scheduled caste, in his dissenting note, had suggested modification of the common list of socially and educationally backward classes, prepared by the Tata Institute of Social Studies, by identifying forward castes among them. Fears have been raised in a number of quarters that this class, by virtue of being socially and educationally forward among the other backward classes (OBCs), would hog all the benefits. Naik said the higher castes or 'intermediate backward classes' had made their presence felt in the caste hierarchical society, either by their numerical strength or their age-old co-existence with other advanced communities in villages and towns. The 'depressed backward classes', on the other hand, being extremely backward, socially, educationally as well as economically, would be incapable of availing of the opportunity accorded by the Mandal Commission's report, the dissent note said. 'It would take concerted efforts at the national level', Naik noted, 'by way of sagacious inputs of safeguards, so that benefits of reservation could percolate to them in a large measure. Noting Naik's dissent while presenting the report, B.P. Mandal said the suggestion to treat this most deprived and under-privileged sections of backward classes as a separate entry was not acceptable to the Commission. Rejecting the suggestions, Mandal felt they would result in a situation repugnant to Article 15(4) of the Constitution, which pertains to reservation for socially and educationally backward classes of people. In addition, he said, the population figures of the depressed backward classes worked out by Naik were very arbitrary and based on pure conjecture. In his minute of dissention, Naik also criticised the Constitution for failing to postulate in it the depressed backward classes. This, he said, resulted in serious constraint in establishing an egalitarian society based on justice, social, economic and political. Even today, he noted, members of this segment of society continued to submit to their fate rather than evoke their rights granted under the Constitution.

Moreover, Naik said, intermediate backward classes perpetrated the treatment they themselves received at the hands of the upper castes, against the 'depressed backward classes.' The 1931 Census showed that out of 43.70 per cent Hindu backward classes groups classified in the main report, depressed backward classes made up 25.56 per cent. Thus, he said though from the population point of view the two groups were equal, disparity between them was vast. Naik recommended to the Commission that 15 per cent of the 27 per cent reservation for backward classes may be set aside for the 'depressed backward classes'. For all other concessions, he said, they should be treated on a par with the scheduled castes and Tribes. The classification suggested by Naik is more relevant to the North Indian States, where not even a small percentage of reservation has been reaching the socially and educationally backward classes of people.

Wrong Assumption

Though the Mandal Commission bears the nomenclature of 'Backward Classes Commission' its report does not define the term 'class' and assumes, quite innocently, that class means caste. The Constitution does not make caste as the basis of reservation; what it talks about is educational and economic backwardness. Mandal, however, believed that 'the substitution of caste by economic test will amount to ignoring the genesis of, social backwardness of the Indian society'. In other words, in his hand 'class' became caste. 'Class' is a socio-economic phenomenon and admits of mobility, while caste is static, and is determined by an ascriptive factor like birth. The Supreme Court of India has; rightly, refused to treat caste as the sole basis of reservation unless it is a scheduled caste for which reservation is a constitutional obligation. In its decision in *State of Madras* v. *Champkam Dorairajan*, the Supreme Court of India held the opinion that the government action in regard to reservation of posts is invalid on the ground that it was based on religion, race and caste only. The Court rejected the agrument of the State based on Article 46 which enjoins on it to make special provisions for the educational and economic interests of the weaker sections of the people on the ground that the fundamental rights were 'sancrosanct and not liable to be abridged by Legislature or Executive act or order except to the extent provided in the appropriate article in Part III. In our opinion, this is the correct way in which the provisions found in Parts III and IV have to be understood'.[3] In other words, caste was not to be the sole criterion for determining backwardness even thsough B.R. Ambedkar was emphatic and said 'what are called backward classes are nothing else but a collection of certain castes'.[4]

A Fallible Document

It is not unusual to find poor people even amongst those who may have been born in upper castes. Similarly, certain individuals belonging to disadvantaged groups have worked their way up the social hierarchy and improved their economic lot under the successive Five Year Plans of development are also as a consequence of the State's policy of job reservation practised since the inception of the Constitution in 1950. In other words, the historically determined caste system has not remained immune to the impulses and energies released by the on-going processes of democracy and development. The doctrine of reservation in the public service is insensitive to the changes taking place since the enforcement of the Constitution. This makes it a fallible document.

From the reservation system in the public services flow several meaningful consequences. One is its impact on efficiency in administration. A widely prevalent view is that those who enter the civil service through the lowered standards bring rather lower levels of efficiency in administration with its deleterious impact on policy-making and implementation. Secondly, the soft corridor of recruitment keeps society deprived of the services of the most competent persons who would otherwise be getting into public administration. This is apt to create heart-burning among the different sections of society. This will also result in resentment which some day may threaten to tear apart the social fabric. Thus viewed, the Mandal Commission Report is a potentially explosive one which may disrupt the social peace. Thirdly, which is far worse, while India is formally committed to the abolition of caste system, the reservation system perpetuates it, which is banal. Today, instead of caste being on the decline in society it is tending to become part of India's psyche even in metropolitan cities. Caste has been India's historic curse, and it is this which is striking deeper and deeper roots and becoming the focus of loyalty under the policy of reservation. The policy of job reservation has thus produced an unintended consequence of fragmenting the country along caste lones. All political parties are seen to exploit caste sentiments during elections, and their stands and utterances are getting more and more caste-oriented. In several parts of the country, caste-based organisations have already started springing up, and, in States like Tamil Nadu, have even struck roots. They act as pressure groups to extract more concessions for them or safeguard what they have already gained — all in the name of social justice. In Tamil Nadu, 50 per cent of the jobs are reserved for the backward castes, 18 per cent for the scheduled castes and scheduled tribes, and the balance 32 per cent of the posts only are availabe for open competition, that is, merit.

Gujarat-style Backlash

While dealing with reservation in the public services, the Constitution of India wants the claims of the target sections of society to be taken into consideration consistently with 'the maintenance of efficiency of administration'. Of late, the efficiency of public administration is getting consistently ignored and bypassed in the quest for vote. This quest is assuming the proportions of a mania on the part of the political parties. The immediate future is likely to see a further extension of reservation facilities to new groups. This trend is bound to lead to a backlash of the Gujarat style. When the Congress Government Chief Minister Madhavsinh Solanki announced in early January 1985 that the reserved quota for the backward castes in universities and government employment in Gujarat would be raised from 10 to 28 per cent, in addition to the 21 per cent already reserved for the scheduled castes and scheduled tribes it unleashed large-scale riots in the State by the anti-reservationists resulting in the killing of some 225 persons and an estimated Rs.2,200 crores worth damages.

The policy of job reservation may also be criticised on the ground that it exhibits precisely the kind of injustice (favouring someone on grounds irrelevant to the purpose) that it is supposed to overcome. It must not be prolonged interminably. The present reservation arrangements have developed powerful vested interests around them, which may thwart reform measures. India's goal of creating a casteless society demands eschewing caste and its replacement by economic criterion.

It has been observed that the policy of reservation is nothing new or novel in India; and in this respect the practice of southern States like Tamil Nadu, Karnataka, Kerala etc., where job reservation has been a long standing practice, are cited. It is then argued that its extension at the level of Central Government is nothing unusual or uncommon. This is an absolutely untenable view, and may be dismissed easily. In the first place a departure from merit as the true base of public recruitment is indefensible everywhere as a general policy, being an indication of an ascriptive age and can never be supported. In India, the local levels of government have always succembed to narrow, clannish pressures and thus constituted no ideal arrangements. But the Central Government has not allowed itself to be susceptible to such clannish thoughts. Rather, the Central Government in India has always been a modern government; progressive in its orienting values and resistant to any form of parochialism. It is this which is to receive a setback under the policy of reservation. More than physical damage to the quality of the public administration, the Mandal schema would have debilitating centrifugal influence on nation-making processes,

NOTES

1. National Front: *Lok Sabha Elections Manifesto 1989*, p. 36.
2. See *Patriot*, December 21, 1989.
3. A.I.R. 1951, SC 226.
4. Quoted in the *Report of the Second Backward Classes Commission*, Part-II, p. 3.

CHAPTER THREE

Mandal and the Post-Mandal

The National Front, in its election manifesto, had mentioned the implementation of the 'Mandal Report', but the timing of its acceptance by the government came as a complete surprise to all including even the MPs of the ruling Janata Dal. Surely, Ram Vilas Paswan, a Cabinet Minister in the V.P. Singh Government, was all the time lobbying for the acceptance of the Mandal Report, but no one apparently expected such an early action.

A most convincing interpretation of V.P. Singh's move on the Mandal Report was the Deputy Prime Minister, Devi Lal's dismissal from the government and his call for a mass rally on 9 August 1990, at the Boat Club in Delhi. Feeling politically insecure, V.P. Singh was seriously planning to take the wind out of Devi Lal's sails, and the Mandal Commission Report came handy to him. Devi Lal, one may note, had his following among even the backward castes, and Singh calculated that Lal would be deflated if he (V.P. Singh) could be perceived as the champion of the backward communities.

Two days before the rally, on 7 August 1990, V.P. Singh threw a bomb-shell over the entire nation by announcing the government's acceptance of the Mandal Report in Parliament. He announced that a reservation of 27 per cent was to be made for the socially and educationally backward classes and that was to be applicable to the services under the Central Government and its public undertakings. His *suo moto* statement in both the Houses of Parliament on 7 August 1990 said

> 'I am happy today to announce in this august House a momentous decision of social justice that my government has taken regarding the socially and educationally backward classes on the basis of the Mandal Commission report.

Members are aware that the Constitution which we gave to ourselves 40 years ago envisages that socially and educationally backward classes be identified, their difficulties removed and their conditions improved in terms of Article 340(1) read with Article 14(4) as well as Article 16(4). It is a negation of the basic structure of our Constitution that till now this requirement was not fulfilled.

The Second Backward Classes Commission under the chairmanship of B.P. Mandal which was appointed on 1 January 1979, submitted its report on 31 December 1980. In accordance with our commitment before the people we included this in our Action Plan. After examining various aspects of it, I am glad to announce that my government has taken the following decisions on the Mandal Commission's Report.

In order to avail ourselves of the benefit of the long experience of a number of States in preparing lists of socially and educationally backward classes and in order to ensure harmonious and quick implementation, we have decided to adopt, in the first phase, the castes common to both the Mandal list as well as the State lists.

The percentage of reservation for the socially and educationally backward classes will be 27 per cent. This reservation will be applicable to services under the Government of India and public undertakings.'

The Prime Minster further said:

'Members are aware that on 14 April at the official function organised to celebrate the birthday of Bharat Ratna Baba Saheb B.R. Ambedkar at the Ambedkar Stadium, I announced the commencement of the Ambedkar Centenary Year and designated it as the 'Year of Social Justice'.

We have taken a number of measures of social justice pertaining to the scheduled castes and scheduled tribes and other weaker sections like removal of injustice done to neo-Buddhists, vesting of Constitutional status and substantial powers in the National Commission for the scheduled castes and scheduled tribes, according due but long-delayed honours to Ambedkar, and so on.

The present decisions are in the same line and belong to the tradition of this government's dedication to the cause of the scheduled castes, scheduled tribes, socially and aducationally backward classes and other weaker sections'.

A Bomb-shell

V.P. Singh's announcement was, as already said, nothing short of a bomb-shell. Initially, the major political parties felt totally non-plussed and dazed, apparently not knowing how to react. Immediate opposition to such a 'benign gift' to a large chunk of Indian society is apt to rob political parties of a vote-bank; and no party, howsoever marginally effective, is prepared to take the risk of losing the game. Therefore, it was only after some days of deliberations that the parties began to criticise the government's decision as hasty and ill-considered and casteist. To no avail. Waiving aside all criticisms, the V.P. Singh Government blissfully proceeded with the task of implementing 27 per cent reservation in the Central Government and public undertakings under it. Within a week of the announcement in the Lok Sabha, it issued an order enforcing the 27 per cent reservation. The office memorandum dated the 13 August 1990, states.

> 'In a multiple undulating society like ours, early achievement of the objective of social justice as enshrined in the Constitution is a must. The Second Backward Classes Commission called the Mandal Commission was established by the then government with this purpose in view, which submitted its report to the Government of India on 31 December 1980.
>
> The government have carefully considered the report and the recommendation of the Commission in the present context regarding the benefits to be extended to the socially and educationally backward classes (SEBC) as opined by the Commission and are of the clear view that at the outset certain weightage has to be provided to such classes in the services of the Union and their public undertakings. Accordingly orders are issued as follows:
>
> (i) 27 per cent of the vacancies in civil posts and services under the Government of India shall be reserved for SEBC.
>
> (ii) The aforesaid reservation shall apply to vacancies to be filled by direct recruitment. Detailed instructions relating to the procedure to be followed for enforcing reservation will be issued separately.

(iii) Candidates belonging to SEBC recruited on the basis of merit in an open competition on the same standards prescribed for the general candidates shall not be adjusted against the reservation quota of 27 per cent.

(iv) SEBC would comprise in the first phase the castes and communities which are common to both the lists in the report of the Mandal Commission and the State Goverenments' lists. A list of such castes/communities is being issued separately.

(v) The aforesaid reservation shall take effect from 7 August 1990. However, this will not apply to vacancies where the recruitment process has already been initiated prior to the issue of these orders.

Similar instructions in respect of public sector undertakings and financial institutions including public sector banks will be issued by the Department of Public Enterprises and the Ministry of Finance respectively.'

A dazed nation took some time to realise the far-reaching implications of the announcement. And when the reaction came, it was on an unprecedented scale. Broadly speaking, the subsequent events followed two paths. One was mounting demand for extension of similar facilities to other uncovered groups in society, and the government's increasing readiness also to accommodate them. The second was the emergence of a firmer and determined resistance to the Mandal recommendations, viewing the Mandal Report as vicious capable of plunging India into a perpetual castewar. Soon the symptom surfaced.

All kinds of groups of people in the society began making demands for extension of these facilities to them. It may be noted that the Muslim members of the Rajya Sabha made a strong demand that their community get preferential treatment in matters of public employment over and above its those sections which were covered by the recommendations of the Mandal Commission. To this demand, V.P. Singh replied that his government was 'not averse' to reserving jobs. But that would need all-party consensus since[2] a constitutional amendment was necessary, he added.

The second path on which the events travelled was marked by an increasing consolidation of informed public opinion against the quota system and resistance to the governmental move. As soon as the V.P. Singh Government announced the reservation of 27 per cent of government jobs for backward castes virtually all the forces of modernisation in the society woke up and mobilised themselves against the ante-deluvian stance of the government. Students were the first to react sharply and start agitation to be soon joined by teachers. Nearly all professional circles lost no time in criticising the measure. The mass media (except the electronic media which is under state control) was equally loud and unambiguous in pointing out the dangerous implications of reservation policy in public recruitment. So destabilising was the policy announcement of V.P. Singh that news papers brought out editorials saying that V.P. Singh's measure was designed to get political mileage even though he thoughtlessly divided the Indian society along caste-lines and introduced caste war in the society. Intellectuals were shocked. In short, the general opinion was that V.P. Singh showed his utter immaturity and short-sightedness as a statesman and a nation-builder by recognising caste as the base of social re-structuring.

To stop the showballing of the popular agitation against reservation for OBCs, V.P. Singh later made two announcements. The reservation policy of twenty-seven per cent for OBCs was not to be extended to educational institutions. Second, the reservations would continue for 10 years at the end of which it would be reviewed. These constitute a departure from the Mandal Report: the latter wanted reservation in educational institutions also and recommended 20 years of duration (that is, one generation). Such assurances are in the nature of time-gaining devices. A measure like reservation, even when made time-bound in the beginning, breeds powerful vested interests in its favour, which makes it virtually self-perpetuating. Take a case of this kind. Reservations for the scheduled castes and the scheduled tribes were originally designed for ten years only. In practice, it is everytime extended; and though forty years have elapsed, these continue in no diminishing way. One may take a leaf out of Tamil Nadu's experience in this area. Job reservation was first started in old Madras Presidency as early as the twenties of the present century but these are still continuing. Rather reservation is enlogised and publicised as a model of social engineering. What is more, its end is not in sight: indeed, not a word has been uttered suggesting its termination now or at a future date. Social concessions, once initiated, get taken for granted and their continuation is seldom questioned.

Janata Party: The Emerging Support Structure

Adult franchise and periodic general election have, in a real sense, contained the potential of a time-bomb capable of unleashing nothing short of revolutionary changes in the Indian political structure and its culture. Ever since 1952 when the first general election took place, a change, even though becoming more clearly manifested only after an interval of time, began taking place in a subtle way in the power structure of the Indian democracy. This was happening through a highly traditional channel: the caste system. The electoral system of the country has transformed the character of India's traditional caste system. Election's began using caste for vote-mobilisational purposes, first shyly and later openly and loudly. In this process, the original objective of the caste system was getting weakened and becoming less and less relevant; and the political system was discovering its new use. Castes began to be used as vote-banks. In other words, the castes were getting updated.

The upper castes, always numerically small in numbers, were, as result, losing their hegemony and an obvious shift of power was occurring in the society. The early seventies witnessed a sure emergence of what are called intermediate castes as principal contenders of political power at the State level in many States. This caste-alliance began to be known by the name of AJGAR. AJGAR stands for *A*hirs, *J*ats, *G*ujars and *R*ajputs. When *M*uslims are added to this combination of socio-political forces, it becomes MAJGAR which was the case at the time of the 1989 election.

With the passage of time, the Hindi belt saw a firm and visible strengthening and consolidation of the caste-alliance of these intermediate castes. Ever since the beginning of socio-economic planning these castes have been gaining in social and economic terms, and having become bolder, they began seeking appropriate accommodation in the country's political system. The present Janata Dal, which is basically a party of north India, is emerging as a political party dominated by these new forces of the Hindi belt though it has a sprinkling of other castes too. This party wanted to expand its political support base; and V.P. Singh, the Prime Minister and a very skilful even if wily politician — which politician is not? — has succeeded in wooing the Muslims in the 1989 election thus making his party MAJGAR: a party mobilising *M*uslims, *A*hirs, *J*ats, *G*ujars and *R*ajput. *R*ajputs, who have been adversely hit by mandalisation, are likely to drop out very shortly.

Admittedly, the Janata Dal is a highly heterogeneous combination not without internal contradictions and its durability too is uncertain. Yet the broad fact is that the present government, which in reality is the Janata Dal Government, other parties being on the extreme frings and rather inconsequential, is utilising the reins of power in strengthening and consolidating the intermediate, now called backward, castes and forging it into a politically viable force in Indian politics — or, to be more correct, in the Hindi belt.

NOTES

1. See *Statesman*, September 1, 1990.
2. While dealing with the same issue, the Minister for Welfare, Ram Vilas Paswan, assured G. G. Swell that the government would not be pressurised into changing its list of minorities.

   Paswan firmly told the BJP members that minorities were established on a national basis — in relation to the overall population and rejected their suggestion that the strength of a community within a particular region be the yardstick. The BJP had argued that the Hindus' in the Kashmir Valley and the North-Eastern States be treated as a minority.

   J. P. Mathur (BJP) contended that under Article 25 of the Constitution, Sikhs were to be bracketed with Hindus — how could the government consider them a minority? Initially Paswan had no answer, but later pointed out that Sikhs had sought legal redress under Article 29 and were now accepted as a minority.

CHAPTER FOUR

Morality of Mandalisation of Public Services

The process of Mandalisation of India's public services has been firmly set into motion with the National Front Government's announcement reserving, for the backward castes, 27 per cent of jobs under the Central Government and public undertakings and a further proposal to set aside 5 to 10 per cent of jobs for the poor 'irrespective of social groups and entirely on the basis of appropriate economic criterion'. These are in addition to the 22.5 per cent of jobs already reserved for the scheduled castes and scheduled tribes. In other words, if reservation for the poor gains acceptance, 54 to 60 per cent of the jobs are to be permanently earmarked for certain specified groups, leaving only about 40 per cent or so for the general category of the candidates. The country's political style and culture being what it is, the government is not likely to trace back its step and reverse its decision about twenty-seven per cent reservation for backward castes, even when, by a single stroke, it has tragically fragmented the society and divided it along narrow, irrelevant caste lines.

The National Front Government has been tirelessly swearing by its election manifesto, taking comfort from the high rate of implementation of its electoral pledges. This line of thinking grievously lacks a tenable moral base — in more senses than one. In the first place, the present regime is a minority one even when all its coalitional partners get counted as a single unit. It has not received society's mandate, either explicit or implicit, to implement its manifesto unilaterally without sounding the various cross-sections of society and developing a broadbased national consensus. It all the more ill-suits a government which, until recently, was talking about value-based politics and a National Government at the Centre. What to say about wider public debate, the decision on reservation for the backward castes was taken without any discussion even within its constituent units, much less within the Janata Dal. Clearly, little justification existed for the seemingly indecent haste in announcing a decision on a momentous issue such as the reservation of jobs. Even, if V.P. Singh's motivation was, as is being rumoured, to outwit Devi Lal, a short-range political gain was sought to be achieved by a measure which has irreparably and unforgivably undermined the basic unity and cohesion of the society.

One should also look at how an election manifesto in India is ordinarily compiled. As is common knowledge, no political party has within itself ably endowed research wings and as such the party platform is hastily composed without an intelligent public discussion, it being no better than a list of broad intentions. The hastiness with which the National Front's own manifesto was prepared is evident from the internal inconsistencies or duplication the document suffers from. It promises 'right to work' to every citizen. If every individual in the country is guaranteed a job where lies the point, then, in reservation of jobs for a particular caste-cluster?

An Ante-diluvian Report

The Mandal Report is ante-diluvian. In order to look objective, the Mandal Commission got a survey research carried out. The research methodology the Mandal Commission adopted was highly deficient and unreliable. The Commission did not survey even 1 per cent of India's total population. It covered only two villages and one urban block in each district. What is more, it received not more than 1872 replies from the whole country. Even the Commission admitted: 'This survey has no pretensions to being a piece of academic research. Throughout this survey our approach has been conditioned by practical considerations, realities of field conditions, constraints of resources and trained manpower and paucity of time. All these factors obviously militate against the requirements of a technically sophisticated and academically satisfying operation'. Read in the light of Roy-Burman's observations, (cited later in the chapter) the research base sought to be provided by Mandal is totally spurious and unreliable. What is more, the Mandal Commission recommendations provide no evidence of use made of the study (more about it later). The fact is that Mandal Report is, at best, an unreliable document. Its compilation of backward castes is very much on the higher side, and is based on no consistent principles. Its computation of total population's 52 per cent as the population of the backward castes is absolutely speculative: the Census of India eschews caste in its enumeration. Immensely more important, Mandal's caste-based reservation assumes that the caste hierarchy is also the economic hierarchy in society. This is, today, fallacious, even if it was true at some time in the past: both democracy and development have permanently delinked the nexus. Today, caste alone is not the determinant of one's location on society's economic ladder. To put it differently, both poverty and affluence refuse to correspond with Mandal-contrived logic of the caste hierarchy. The enumeration of occupation-based castes in the category of backward castes is equally wrong: castes, today, do not correspond with their traditional occupations, thanks to increasing occupational mobility in society.

It is, moreover naive to believe that India's economic problems would be solved by reserving jobs in public administration and increasing the latter's size. A bourgeoning public bureaucracy is itself a cause of the country's travail; and the national policy ought to be to prune it and this too drastically. Even otherwise, no government, even of an affluent society, is able to provide jobs under it to everyone in society. What the State should do, and is capable of doing, is to expand the opportunities of gainful work to the people at large. In other words, avenues for earning an honourable livelihood should be created outside the State, and the latter must not induce people to become overdependent on it for employment.

Employment of Consultants

Mention has been made earlier in a foregoing paragraph of the commissioning of a research in a bid to make the Mandal Report scientific. The Commission, however, did not make any use of the research findings which is confirmed by the person directly involved, B.K. Roy-Burman who headed the Technical Committee and chaired the Research Planning Panel for the Mandal Commission. He says that the report is totally without scientific basis. It exaggerates the number of 'other backward classes', ignores every suggesstion that the experts associated with it made. 'We were used', observed Roy-Burman, whose name figures in the Preface to the Report, along with two other social scientists. 'They associated our names with the Report without listening to us or even consulting us on the basis for their ultimate findings.'

Roy-Burman, who has been the Deputy Registrar-General, Census

Operations, says that Mandal's men sabotaged the expert's suggestions at every stage. To start with, the experts did not want caste to be the basis for identifying backward classes. And finally, they were not even shown the processed data on which the findings hinged. 'We don't know whether the findings were based on the survey, or personal impression or plain imagination', said Roy-Burman. Even the Home Minister of the day was unable to show him the data, he says. When the Mandal Commission first started its proceedings, the experts were asked to determine the criteria that would decide backwardness. They were asked to design the survey.

'Caste was not a satisfactory measure of backwardness. We were more inclined to consider occupations as a measure. Or perhaps, a mix of the two' he says.

A pilot survey was conducted in Birbhum district of West Bengal, taking this mixed approach. The result was startling: only two occupations were truly backward — blacksmiths and potters. They also coincided, roughly, with particular castes. After this, the tampering began. The experts had come up with a system of weightages for various criteria of backwardness. The Commission dumped all these and came up with its own weightages. The experts were not even told about this. 'We had suggested a spectrum of 'weightages' for literacy. Obviously, you cannot equate a person who can barely sign his name with a post-graduate and club them both as literate. This is precisely what the Commission did.'

'If you go just by the literacy rate, many castes become backward. The literacy level among the Jats, this way, is not very different from *dhobis*. But the Jats have many more post-graduates. The system that the Commission adopted is unscientific. It multiplies the number of the backward classes.'

After that, says Roy-Burman, the experts were given a complete go-by. The occupation-caste mix concept was shelved. Mandal wanted caste to be the sole criterion.

The experts did not know whether their survey design was being used. They were not consulted. The experts wanted 151 tables to be made for the purpose of calculation and illustration. But Mandal arbitrarily reduced this number to just 31. 'The Commission was in a hurry to wind up its proceedings. The government had changed and it was, perhaps, not feeling very secure about its future', says Roy-Burman.

'The Commission wanted him to approve its own format. It said there was a time constraint.' The Commission got its own back by refusing to show the social scientists the processed data. 'I wrote to the Commission to tell them that we had been used. The data had to be shown to us. The Commission had to hear our suggestions, though it could over-rule them.' At this stage, the Commission finally told the experts where they stood. 'We have been very cooperative with you. You are being unnecessarily strident,' the Commission wrote back. And the Commission went ahead and published the Report. And the experts were acknowledged for their contributions in the Preface itself. But they were never shown the processed data.

Roy-Burman says: 'I went and met P. C. Sethi who was the Home Minister then, and asked him for the data. I told him that if it had been processed, it should be shown to me.' Even the Home Minister was not able to show Roy-Burman the data on which the fate of the nation is now being decided. 'I still have not seen that data. After all, I want to know how much of the report is based on data, how much on impressions and how much on imagination', he says. He finds Mandal's projection on the 1931 data unscientific. 'There has been so much social mobility since then.' But there is another more serious objection. Roy-Burmon says that many of the castes specified in the 1931 Census are just 'synonyms'. In other words, the same caste has been mentioned separately, according to its name, the name of the community, the name of the occupation, etc. 'There is a lot of duplication. It will just multiply the number of castes that are now called 'other backward classes'.' But none of these views were heard by the man whose report is now law.[1]

The above is a warning to the society. Social research has several motivations behind it. It may be used for ornamental purposes also — to impart legitimacy and sanctity to the pre-conceived views of the managers. In other words, the outside social scientists may just be hired for giving a colour of objectivity and impartiality to local biases and prejudices.

It, thus, flows from the foregoing that the Mandal Commission was not ethical in its motivations and strategy. Indeed, its Report is a model of how a commission on matters of social concern ought not to function.

NOTE

1. See *Indian Express*, August 31, 1990.

CHAPTER FIVE

Mandalisation of Public Services: The Correct Strategy

It would have been prudent for the national policy-makers to have first obtained the feedback from the already operating reservation system for the scheduled castes and scheduled tribes and ploughed it into planning for its extension to other groups of people. This unfortunately has not been done.

It is common knowledge that the benefits of reservation made available since Independence have not percolated to all the levels and sectors of the target groups, which explains the deficiency of these arrangements. Indeed, the bulk of the benefits have been cornered by a few select castes, and the remaining ones have largely or substantially remained where they were. To be more correct, even in these benefit-scoring castes, an elite group has emerged and the benefits of reservation mostly circulate among its members. The same askewed pattern is liable to be reflected in the case of the backward castes also. The three thousand seven hundred and odd castes are not internally homogeneous, being at different levels of development — social, economic, cultural, educational. In such a context, the reserved posts would get hogged in substantial numbers, by the 'forward' among the backward castes. Thus, the reservation for the backward castes would result in the emergence of a few enclaves of affluence among them without serving the intended purpose. Besides, the reservation for the scheduled castes and scheduled tribes was, wisely, a time-bound concession made for a period of 10 years only. But powerful vested interests have emerged and it has in practice become self-perpetuating, being extended continuously. It is also to be noted that reservation at the stage of recruitment is itself perceived as an injustice to society, but its extension to the area of promotion has proved to be extremely harmful to intra-personal relationship and destructive of organisational harmony.

These mistakes must not be repeated when extending the benefits and concessions to new groups. Caste system is peculiar to the Hindus: no other religion suffers from such an encumbrance. For some time, avoidable distortions have been caused to the system of reservation; and caste-based benefits have been extended to other religions also. A cancer is to be contained and tought: it must not be spread. One must also note that the Mandal Report is a lobbyist's report, and is thus an unreliable document. Its list of no fewer than 3,743 backward castes is, highly exaggerated and thus warrants closer scrutiny. Several professional or occupational groups have been included as backward castes, which is untenable.

The case-history of reservation for scheduled castes and tribes shows that pressures would build-up for increasing its percentage in future — in proportion to the population. it is very likely to be demanded in the field of personnel promotion also. The social effort would be increasingly directed towards governmental to gain entry into the category of backward castes, and the pressure for this would be unceasing. Under the logic of reservation, caste-oriented activities would increase and operate in different directions. The backward castes would strive for the status of scheduled castes; and general category castes would press for their recognition as backward ones. This is a human nature. In the period when no reservation culture existed in Indian public administration, the so-called lower castes were trying to move up socially and to enhance their social status. The following observation in the Census Report of 1921 is instructive:

> 'The opportunity of the census was . . . seized by all but the highest castes to press for recognition of social claims and to secure, if possible, a step upwards in the social ladder. This attitude has been strengthened by the recent development of caste sabhas, or societies whose purpose is to advance the position and welfare of the caste'. Recognition of caste for social action is apt to spawn up caste-fuelled politics with all its dangerous consequences.

'Means' Test to be the Basis

Poverty, it must be noted, is becoming less and less respector of the caste hierarchy, and one cannot rule out the emergence of affluence among sections of the backward castes. Such people who are economically well-off must at all cost be kept excluded from the category of beneficiaries. This suggests adoption of a suitable 'means' test before benefits of reservation become available.

To drive home his point, individuals who are in the category of tax-payers may be completely kept out of the benefits. This will ensure that the income really needy have access to the concessions. Further, the number of chances for getting the caste-based concession including concession to the scheduled castes and scheduled tribes should be restricted so that there is a proper spread of the beneficiaries. Chance-restriction, to repeat, is absolutely necessary. Finally, the duration of the concessions should be fixed at 10 years and must not at any cost be extended beyond this period. One should also utter a word of warning at this stage. Many more groups have already started mounting demands on the government for extending reservation benefits to them. These must be firmly resisted.

One word more. So long as caste remains on the national cognitive map of India the unity and cohesion of the country would remain drastically impaired. In other words, nation-making process is liable to remain impeded when caste remains recognised, even indirectly, as the basis of State action. Rather, the purpose of ameliorating the lot of the backward communities should be better served by strengthening the country's educational system and providing quality education to all in society including the members of what are today called backward castes scheduled castes and tribes. All in society should attend the same system of education regardless of the earning capacity or economic status. This will produce a society which would be psychologically and emotionally homogeneous and well-knitted. In 1947, we got 'India' from the hands of the colonial rulers. Since then, the challenge has been to make Indians out of us — who are basically Punjabis, Bengalees, Gujaratis, or Brahmins, Thakurs, Jats, Yadavs, Reddys, Khammas, etc. Mandalisation and Indianity cannot go together: the former is a centrifugal force while the latter is a centripetal one.

Unfortunately, the country is presently in the grip of short-range politicians, and in the currently prevelant frenzied environment this plea for the total displacement of caste has a remote chance of winning acceptance. But the fact is that education is the true antidote to backwardness. Indeed, it would be appropriate to have the entire philosophy and practice of reservation in India reviewed in a comprehensive, objective way keeping in mind the tasks of nation-making, state-building and development.

To make the public services in India more broad-based in composition and representative in character, the Mandal's is not the wise course of action. Rather, it will be in the lasting interest of India if caste is physically as well as psychologically banished form the country's social and political lexicons no less than orientations and behaviour. The society should provide for high quality education to the weaker sections and even economically support them. Pre-civil service examination coaching should be organised on a large scale. In other words, the solution of lower representation of a large number of groups in the society should be devised within the framework of the country's goal of a casteless society. In short, while criticising the Mandal Report, the intention is not to perpetuate the *status quo*. Far from it. At present, the higher civil service in India has a narrow social base. Speaking in casteist terms, it has a preponderance of Brahmins and Kayasthas. This must be broadened by universalising and toning up the educational system in the land and by expanding the middle class through acceleration of the economic development processes. In all countries, the higher civil service has middle class predominance, and it is only through the expansion of the middle class that a more representative bureaucracy emerges.

Aftermath of the Mandal Report

Finally, acceptance of the Mandal Commission recommendation of 27 per cent reservation of jobs in the Central Government and public undertakings for the backward castes is unlikely to give peace to the V.P. Singh Government and to its successor governments. Job-reservation is apt to create a host of problems on a continuing basis. Some of the major issues which would arise in the wake of the governmental acceptance may be referred to very briefly in what follows. To qualify for the 'backward caste' concessions, a certificate is necessarily to be required by the government. Such a certificate is not very difficult to get at present, thanks to the low level of public morality in the public services. One has merely to pay a fixed 'fee' to an elected representative or a district level public functionary to get it and become 'backward'. In the second place, the Mandal Commission has categorised as many as 3,743 castes as backward in contrast to 2,399 identified by the first Backward Classes Commission (1953). Despite this dose of extravagant generosity, more and more castes would clamour for inclusion in the beneficiaries' list, and this would generate unending conflict in the society.

Thirdly, as the backward castes themselves not homogeneous socially, economically and educationally, most jobs would inevitably be hogged by a few castes – or to be more correct, by the elite among the better placed castes. A demand for fixation of sub-quotas for each or cluster of backward castes is likely to be made under the name of 'real' social justice.

The present work makes one feel a bit uncertain if not cynical about the public services' immediate future. To relieve the tension on the mind of the reader, a couple of musings are not here completely uncalled for. It has been said that an important event has an innate knack of repeating itself — first as a tragedy, and second time as a farce. What about the 'second time'. Let one speculate about the future shape of things. The term 'backward' is not an elegant expression. A demand is likely to be made made for a better term. Just as backward countries became developing nations, the backward castes may demand a term like developing castes for themselves. One thing more. Backward castes have yet to discover an 'arch-saint' for themselves as at present they have none. Who is to fill the bill is yet uncertain. Kansi Ram, the president of the Bahujan Samaj Party, is a likely candidate along with Ram Vilas Paswan and Sharad Yadav. Simultaneously, in future a demand is likely to be made to confer Bharat Ratna on B.P. Mandal, the chairman of the Commission which recommended the 27 per cent reservation. His birth anniversary may be celebrated as a national holiday in the not too distant future.

Some Concerns for the Society

The case-study of the Mandal Commission and its triumph raises a few issues for which a cultured society should find satisfactory answers. It is difficult to recall any other public issue which has aroused so much social controversy even bordering on acute acrimony as the Mandal scheme of job reservation. The Mandal Report has vertically divided the society in India. What is more, the cleavages thus created are neither temporary nor shortlived. The issue is about the extent to which a government in a democracy could go in the matter of making public policies. Democracy implies a level of sensitivity to the other views even though it entrusts the task of governance to a particular party based on majority — or to any other minority in a minority government. Democracy has its boundaries, setting a definite limit to the rulers' options and choices. In India, the V.P. Government has shown stubbornly inflexible attitude on the Mandal Report even though the opposition to it is widespread and stiff. A government elected for a five-year term has little moral right to fetter and handicap the society indefinitely by its myopic actions. In other words, the society will have to devise ways of obliging a government to evolve and internalise norms of understanding,politeness and circumspection. Controlling the arrogance and obstinacy of the politician is a major problem for the society.

There is a second issue demanding an answer. Political parties, one may note, emerged as ideologically motivated entities but with the passage of time they have been becoming more and more of mere election fighting organisations with the eye wholly set on winning at the hustings, thus giving a short shift to ideology or long range interests of the society. Today, a political party loves speaking pleasing things to different groups in a bid to mobilise as many votes as possible. It, therefore, comes about that all parties are seen to take up populist measures; and in the process concerns of future, necessarily of no populist nature, such as nation-building tasks, remain unsupported, more so in a fragmentation-oriented polity like India. Theoretically, job reservation — a denial and negation of merit — is indefensible. But when the agitation against the Mandal Report started no political party was prepared to condemn it openly and directly for the fear of alienating the vote banks. The question is: What is the true role of a political party? Just to be populist? To do what ever it likes just to remain in political power even though the nation may be destroyed by its actions? It is the appropriate time for the nation to think about suitable checks and balances on the political parties of the land too.

CHAPTER SIX

Kaka Kalekar's Views

Kaka Kalelkar had his profound apprehensions about caste-based job reservation in India's public administration. His views are expressed in the letter which he wrote to the President of India while forwarding the Report of the Backward Classes Commission (1953-55).

GOVERNMENT OF INDIA

Backward Classes Commission

New Delhi 2, 30 March 1955

Revered President,

It is with a mixed sense of joy, anxiety and relief, that I submit to you the Report of the Backward Classes Commission. You were pleased to appoint the Commission on the 29 January 1953, but formally inaugurated it on the 18 March 1953. It took us full two long years to finish our labours and prepare the Report. We did our best to present a unanimous Report, and I am glad to say that the major portion of our recommendations has been almost unanimous. From the very complexity of our task, it was inevitable that there should be differences of opinion even on fundamental matters. It should be a matter of agreeable surprise that the members of the Commission were united on so many matters and even where we have felt constrained to hold different views, our anxiety for the welfare of the backward classes and betterment of their condition is not in any way the less. The very minutes of dissent prove this beyond any doubt.

2. I was expected, as Chairman, to prepare the Report of the Commission. I had my notes ready, written out fairly in detail, but I felt that it would be much better and more satisfactory if I allowed my

colleagues to write the report after reading my notes and utilising them to the extent they liked. This task of writing the Report, I left to Shri Mariappa, who has had valuable experience in the administration of the Mysore State. Although he could not devote much time in the beginning to the work of the Commission on account of his preoccupations with the Mysore Congress work, be gave sufficient time, and worked hard in preparing the Report. This rendered my work very easy. I had simply to go over what he wrote, and suggest a few modificaitons here and there. My other colleagues also had their share, and the Report, as it finally emerged must be accepted as the joint production of us all; but, I must express my heartfelt thanks to Shri Mariappa, for the unstinted labour which he devoted on the production of the Report. Dr. Anup Singh helped us to put the report in shape.

Shri Shah, with his knowledge of the Public Service Commission, of public accounts and anthropology was of great help ot us in many ways. It was at his insistence that we could work out our chapter on Grants in detail. The details were chiefly supplied by Shri Patel.

3. We prepared a detailed State-wise Report, and I had expected that it will be the second part of our general report, but we found that it would take too long a time before it was discussed in detail and finalised. Our recommendations, which are the main part of the Report, do not depend upon the State-wise section. We, therefore, towards the end, decided to delete this portion. But, some thought and labour has been bestowed upon this State-wise Reports section — and I would recommend that, although it is not a part of our official report, it may be forwarded to the various States and they might make what use they like of the contents.

It was our intention to prepare a detailed glossary of the various communities recommended by us, for being included in the list of the other backward classes. We received some information from the States and collected some through our Research Section. This information also may be useful, but we found it difficult to go over these and arrive at a uniformity of conclusions. We decided, therefore, to drop this glossary also from our Report, although it would have been a valuable commentary on the lists we have supplied. The Government of India may, with the help of the State Governments and the Commissioner for scheduled castes and scheduled tribes, check, enlarge and complete the glossary that we prepared, and issue it as an official publication. It will help administrators in many ways.

It is evident that government wanted to know the views and

aspirations of the representatives of the backward classes. The very selection of the Members on the Commission indicated this anxiety, and the Report will show that it clearly voices the feelings, fears and aspirations of the present-day leaders of the various backward communities in the various States of India. Backwardness, even in formulating the feelings, fears and aspirations, must be an inevitable characteristic in this matter, and it should not surprise anyone if both these fears and aspirations belong more to the past.

4. The age-old resignation of the masses to their lot is gone. They no longer believe that it is Fate that has kept them backward. They are not yet alive to their own share in the backwardness, *viz.*, apathy, lethargy and negligence. They are too backward to be introspective and to find out what is wrong with themselves. It is but natural and to some extent justifiable that they should find fault with the situation around them, and their eyes should be reveted on the fact of their being exploited by the upper classes. Their representatives and leaders have read the literature that we evolved in finding faults with the evils of the British rule. They have come to know how one race dominates another, and how those who have to suffer have, perforce, to unite against the forces of vested interests. They have heard of the inevitability of class conflict. No wonder if they are prone to draw hasty conclusions.

5. Social reformers from ancient times have always been introspective. Most of them, coming from the upper castes have been most critical of the faults and foibles of their own class and criticised them in unstinted measure, for all the soical neglect and injustice towards the backward classes. All this has combined to help the representatives of the backward classes in preparing a case, and it should not surprise anyone if the case is overdrawn, stereo-typed and fails to recognise the amount of righteousness in the nation expressed in the struggle for social justice carried on by the social leaders through the ages.

6. We have to recognise the painful fact that all the efforts of the social reformers belonging to the upper classes have been more than counter-balanced by the blind-selfishness and traditional self-justificaiton of the upper classes. There is an amount of uneasiness amongst the backward classes. This has been carefully fanned and organised by interested perosns who stand to gain both materially and in leadership by organising discontent.

7. However unpalatable this may be, and however turbid the motives of some of the representatives of the backward classes, no one

can say that they are not justified in complaining that there is an unsympathetic uniformity in the attitude of the majority of the upper classes, from which the backward classes have to suffer.

8. I would plead, therefore, that the case of the backward classes need not be analysed too critically, and it is no use marshalling evidence to prove that the accusations levelled at the upper classes by the backward classes are not substantially correct, and that it is only interested representatives that distort the situation. Even conceding that the whole picture is one-sided and over-drawn, one has to recognise that there is an uneasiness in the minds of the masses, and this uneasiness is gathering momentum.

9. It is unfortunate that the Swaraj Government which is struggling hard to establish social justice has been left to alone for the blind and conservative attitude and the traditional policy of the upper classes, with the result that even though government is prompted with the best of motives, little credit is given to it, and all the evils of the social system are levelled at it. It would be well if representatives of the backward classes remembered that whatever good they find in the Constitution and the liberal policy of the government is the result of the awakened conscience of the upper classes themselves. Whatever the government is doing by way of atonement is readily accepted and acclaimed by the nation as a whole. And let it not be forgotten that the upper classes have contributed their share in formulating the policies of the government. Removal of untouchability, establishment of equality and social justice, special consideration for the backward classes — all these elements found their place in the Constitution without a single dissentient voice form the upper classes.

10. Some people who are unwilling to recognise any good point in their own nation try to expalin this righteousness as a reaction to world opinion. We know how far world opinion counts where self-interest and pride of race are dominant! We know how far world opinion is able to influence the policies of countries like America, South Africa and Portugal! It is not fair to be blind to the awakened conscience of the nation itself in which the upper classes are also honourably included — when recognising the good points in the Constitution, of which we have every reason to be proud.

11. We have now to see if there are any defects in the framework of the Constitution itself, or the policy of the government, by which the enlightened conscience fails sufficiently to organise itself and forces of selfishness, self-aggrandisement and mutual suspicion are often times

allowed to be organised and pitted against each other leading unwittingly to a class conflict. I am led to believe that such defects are present both in the Constitution and in the policy of the government. It is not easy to locate them, but it seems to be a patent fact that forces of opportunism, selfishness, and self-aggrandisement, mutual suspicion and conflict, on both sides, invariably come to the forefront and get organised, whereas the forces of brotherliness, of social justice and gratitude are not allowed or do not get a chance to function with a united will. Unless we feel gratitude for the patience of the long-suffering masses and for their respect for law and order; unless we have gratitude to the best amongst the nation for their struggle for the establishment of righteousness; unless we have gratitude for all that the mahatmas and social reformers have been doing, and unless we feel grateful to Providence for the mysterious way in which it is training the nation for a higher service of humanity, we may not be able to appreciate the forces of good that have been working in our nation, and, through our nation, for the betterment of the lot of humanity.

12. We have found it inevitable to attribute most of the evils of our social condition to caste. We are not blind to the good intentions and wisdom of our ancestors who built the caste structure. It was, perhaps, the only way through which they could teach the nation to forget and rise above racial, clannish, tribal and similar biological groupings of society and to accept a workable arrangement of social existence based on cultural hierarchy and occupational self-government.

13. But whatever the beauty and success of these primitive social experiments of the past, we are sufficiently advanced today towards a feeling of nationhood and national solidarity. We were confronted with the existence of a multiplicity of religions in our land in an age of democracy; we struggled through the situation and have managed to come out successful, however severely mauled and weakened we may have been in the process. We hope now to build a familyhood of races, a familyhood of religions and a familyhood of cultures. We are now beyond the necessity of working on the basis of hierarchy. We have been able to build a feeling of oneness in the whole nation. We have learnt to adjust religious, racial and cultural differences. We have decided to overcome the inequalities based on differences of wealth and intellectual equipment and that by a democratic process of giving equal opportunities to all to attain the highest alike in educational, cultural and economic fields.

14. Natioal solidarity demands that in a democratic set-up the

government recognise only two ends — the individual at one end and the nation as a whole at the other — and that nothing should be encouraged to organise itself in-between these two ends to the detriment of the freedom of the individual and solidarity of the nation. All communal and denominational organisations and groupings of lesser and narrower units have to be watched carefully so that they do not jeopardise the national solidarity and do not weaken the efforts of the nation to serve all the various elements in the body politic with equity.

15. The secular democracy of India gives full freedom to all the established religions of the world to exist and propagate themselves in the land because this, our secular democracy, has equal respect for all of them, of course to the extent that they do not undermine universal brotherhood and respect for the personality of every citizen irrespective of his or her economical, educational or cultural traditions or standpoint. Mutual respect, mutual help and mutual trust are the touchstone on which all communal and denominational activities will be tested, and anything that undermines these fundamental principles of democracy will be exposed and brought to book.

16. It is a hopeful sign of the times and a guarantee for the future well-being of every interest in the nation that the government is fast progressing towards the ideals of a socialistic pattern, and the people themselves are accepting and developing the ideals of Sarvodaya in all the sectors of our national existence. Thus both the nation and the natioal government have accepted the ideal of familyhood of all the nations, all races, of all civilisations and cultures. It is in this context that the conditon of the backward classes in India has to be understood and appreciated, and the remedies suggested are to be systematically applied. The remedies will not yield the desired result within a stipulated period unless there is a nation-wide awakening through systematic propaganda and moral revival, and practical steps are taken both by the government and the people. The old taboos, along with the hierarchical segregation in the matter of food and drink and marriages, have to be overcome. The Bhoodan movement is teaching the whole nation to accept the familyhood of all the people living in this land. It is not merely an equitable redistribution of land between the landed and the landless, but it is a recognition by the nation that we all form one human family and we are responsible for each other's well-being.

17. A similar nation-wide social revolution, not confined to the upper classes, neither only to the Hindus alone, has to be inaugurated.

18. All our social reform movements and the moral fervour behind them are so far generally confined to the Hindus. We have always allowed the Muslim and the Christian communities to have their own way. This may be a good example in toleration; it may perhaps reflect the hope that the reform amongst the Hindus may give rise to a healthy emulation in the minds of other denominations also. But political self-interest has so far come in their way, and orthodoxy amongst the Christians and the Muslims and other denominations is as hopeless and hard as the orthodoxy amongst the Hindus nations is as hopeless and hard as the orthodoxy amongst the Hindus — only, the former is stronger and never discredited. Sometimes the criticism is heard that the government is partial to the Hindus in the sense that it throws its whole weight on the side of social reform amongst Hindus and helps that community to overcome its weakness, but when it comes to any social legislation for overcoming the social defects and antiquated moral standards of non-Hindus, the government has thought it fit to follow a policy of non-intervention and non-interference. This is bound to weaken the nation as a whole, and thereby weaken the forces of moral and spiritual reform started in the Muslim and Christian countries of the world. It is sometimes a wiser course to allow social reform in the minority communities to grow spontaneously from within instead of using the weight of the enlightened sense of the majority community for quickening the pace of refrom amongst them. It is safe to wait for some time at least.

The Backward Amongst the Non-Hindus

19. Being convinced that the upper castes among the Hindus have to atone for the neglect of which they were guilty towards the 'lower' classes, I was prepared to recommend to the government that all special help should be given only to the backward classes and even the poor and the deserving among the upper classes may be safely kept out from the benefit of this special help. My eyes were however opened to the dangers of suggesting remedies on caste basis when I discovered that it is going to have a most unhealthly effect on the Muslim and Christian sections of the nation. It is a patent fact that the bulk of the Muslims and Christians in India are converts from the Hindu fold. This conversion was encouraged by the fact that Islam and Christianity were fundamentally opposed to caste. The 'lower castes' in the Hindu fold left their traditional religion and joined the religion of the ruling race

because they felt assured that in that way they would be free from the tyranny of caste and caste prejudices.

20. For the purpose of the Backward Classes Commission, we could not accept the view that all Indian Christians or all Muslims were backward without accepting the logical conclusion that all Hindus also were in the same sense equally backward. The Govern ent of India recognised certain castes among the Hindus as backward and offered special scholarships, concessions and privileges to these communities. This led the Muslims and Christians also to assert that although their religion was fundamentally different, and that theoretically it is opposed to caste, in practice their society was more or less caste-ridden. The special concessions and privileges accorded to Hindu castes acted as a bait and a bribe inciting Muslim and Christian society to revert to caste and caste prejudices and the healthy social reforms effected by Islam and Christianity were being thus rendered null and void. Muslims came forward to prove that except for the four upper castes, namely, Sheikh, Syed, Moghul and Pathan, all the other Muslim castes were inferior and backward. The Indian Christians also were prepared to fall in the trap. They told the Ministry of Education and the Backward Class Commission that caste is rampant among them. We discovered to our pain and sorrow that untouchability did obtain in the extreme South amongst Indian Christians, and Indian Christians were prepared in many places to assert that they were still guided by caste not only in the matter of untouchability but in social hierarchy of high and low. Their social and religious leaders in thier anxiety to secure some governmental help for their own people supported the contention that caste was rampant among Indian Christians also.

21. This was a rude shock and it drove me to the conclusion that the remedies we suggested were worse than the evil we were out to combat.

22. This painful realisation came to me almost towards the end of our labours. I could not stem the current of opinion within the Commission itself and ultimatley decided, though reluctantly, to side with the majority with whom I had cooperated throughout in formulating remedies on caste basis. It is only when the Report was being finalised that I started thinking a new and found that backwardness could be tackled on a basis or a number of bases other than that of caste. I only succeeded in raising the suspicion of the majority of my colleagues, that I was trying to torpedo the recommendations of the Commission. This was another reason why I

signed the report without even a minute of dissent. We must be able to help both Indian Christians and Muslims without their being driven to accept the fissiparous principle of caste. This will also enable us to remove the bitterness which the extremely poor and helpless amongst the upper class Hindus feel that they are being victimised for no fault of their own. Once we eschew the principle of caste, it will be possible to help the extremely poor and deserving from all communities. Care of course must be taken to give preference to those who come from the traditionally neglected social classes.

Extreme Poverty also leads to Social Backwardness

23. A secular State that does not concern itself with religious differences and has no preference for one religion over another cannot go into the details of the religious prejudices of one section against another. It is only when a community or a group is proved to be working under a special handicap and is not allowed freely to function as citizens, that the State may intervene and make special provision for the advancement of such underprivileged and handicapped communities. It is not enough to prove that one community is regarded as inferior by another. The Christians may look down upon the Jews and the Jews may retaliate with the same feelings. The Brahman may regard the Bania as inferior and the Bania in his turn may regard the Brahman as a mere social dependent. But such opinions and prejudices do not come in the way of the full growth of these communities. This opinion about the inferiority of certain communities has not necessarily retarded the progress of those communities, either educationally or economically. If such communities have neglected education it is because they had no use for it. Now that they have discovered their mistake, it is for them to make the necessary efforts for making up the leeway.

24. They will naturally receive whatever help is available to all citisens, but they can claim no special help because they neglected education in the past. And yet, if these communities are to be regarded as backward and given additional help on a caste basis, the only course open to the State would be to impose a communal tax on the well-to-do members. Whatever money is collected through such a tax may be spent on giving special scholarships and help to the poorer members of those communities.

25. Till recently, good many Communities were organising caste

conferences and collecting funds for granting scholarships to boys and girls of their own community. That was a good lesson in self-help and a good number of communities have thus come forward in material well-being. But now all burden is sought to be thrown on the common exchequer and those who have thoughtlessly neglected education in the past are now seeking preferential treatment in government services. This is anything but fair. It is one thing to help those who have been long neglected and who have no conception of the needs of modern times and who had not the wherewithals with which to educate themselves. Such communities deserve all help, but the richer and well-to-do communities may not neglect their own poor people and throw the burden on the common exchequer, and yet ask for special preferential treatment for even the rich amongst them, so far as government services are concerned.

A general formula of helping all persons, to whatever caste or community they may belong, provided they belong to the special backward class of the extremely poor, covers such cases of extremely poor, who have been cruely neglected by their own community. Families whole income is less than Rs. 800 a year do need special help irrespective of the community to which they belong. Such poor and deserving may even belong either to the upper communities or the educationally backward but otherwise prosperous people of the dominant communities among the backward classes. The extremely poor cannot be denied special help simply because they happen to belong to a particular community.

26. Care, of course, must be taken to see that these do not carry away all State help, and leave the extremely backward communities unattended to. The list of backward communities supplied by us ought to be a guide in all preferences. Unfortunately, we have not been able to supply a regular hierarchy of all the communities residing in India. That, perhaps, would have been the best guide for preference in all governmental concessions and privileges.

Reservation in Services

27. I am definitely against reservation in government services for any community for the simple reason that the services are not meant for the servants but they are meant for the service of society as a whole. Administration must have the services of the best men available in the land and these may be found in all communities. Reservation of posts

for certain backward communities would be as strange as reservation of patients for particular doctors. The patients are not meant to supply adequate or proportionate clientele to all the doctors, whatever their qualifications.

28. The best policy that could be recommended is that given the same or almost the same qualifications, candidates or aspirants from the backward classes should be given a decided preference.

29. Coming to details of governmental services the principle of 'no reservation' but 'generous preference' should be strictly followed in class I (and perhaps in class II also) of services because services belonging to these classes demand higher standards of integrity, efficiency and initiative. It is not suggested that these qualities are the monopoly of any one community or that these qualities are at a discount in the case of other communities. Inferiority complex cultivated by the backward communities leads them to believe that they are, and will always remain, deficient in certain qualities, and therefore they need the backing of reservation. Experience in the past proves that reservations come in the way of healthy emulation and those who learnt to depend upon reservation are, oftentimes, not alert enough to improve their quality. They rest on their privileges and all zest for self-improvement is dulled.

30. But we have to recognise that the tradition of the past so many years, when the British rulers wanted to placate many elements, has created a demand for reservation in government jobs. The scheduled castes and scheduled tribes already enjoy some reservation. It is natural, therefore, that the other backward classes should also desire to have some reservation in their favour.

31. In this matter one clear principle must be accepted and observed. Reservations if contemplated must not exceed 49 per cent, whatever the total population of all the 'Reserved' communities.

32. I believe that in Class I and Class II Services, the backward classes will stand to gain, both morally and materially, if they do not demand a reservation percentage in the vacancies and simply rely on the fair-mindedness of the administration to use their preference in favour of the backward classes. They could then demand the greatest facilities for training and education in order to fit themselves for the highest jobs, as speedily as possible.

33. As regards Class III and Class IV services, it has to be recognised that the policy of preference may not work with equal force. It will take some time before the policy of preference percolates

through the thick layer of indifference and vested interests. I would, therefore, accept 49 per cent for the reservation of seats, all told, for all the backward classes. Candidates from the backward classes can of course compete in the sector of 51 per cent and take any number of seats by sheer worth over and above the reservation. In Class III services, I would have an additional principle of favouring women candidates over men. Most of the clerical posts must, hereafter, go to women, men being expected to work in the fields or trade and industry.

34. In the case of Class IV services, there is an almost cent per cent monopoly of the Bhangi Class for scavenging work. There is already an ample percentage of backward people in class IV. Here I would recommend that the scheduled castes and scheduled tribes and the starred communities from amongst the other backward classes should have a definite preference over others.

35. In Class IV services over and above necessary personal qualification, the recommendation of certain reliable persons is important because much depends upon the loyalty and integrity of this service. The usual practice is to demand that there must be at least two persons who stand guarantee for the honesty, loyalty and regularity of this useful and humble servant. This leads to each man bringing another from his own community because, thus alone can he stand guarantee for the good behaviour of the new man. This principle is healthy enough, but there are wholesale communities amongst the backward classes who have never had a chance of occupying even the post of chaprasis, jamadars and daftries. Such unrepresented communities need special preference.

36. The policy recommended does not preclude the backward classes from entering the sector of service open to general competition. It must be the policy of the government to encourage more and more people from the backward communities to occupy places of responsibility and initiative. The greater the confidence shown to the backward classes, the greater is the security of the State. Therefore, although some of us are unwilling to reserve more percentage of seats for the backward classes, we whole-heartedly recommend to the government that they should do everything in their power to see that men of ability and integrity from amongst the backward classes are given a definite preference, other things being equal; and they are made to feel that the country is theirs and the whole nation has complete confidence in their patriotism and equal love for all sections of the naiton. •

37. In Class III services much depends upon actual experience rather than on initial qualifications. Therefore, we would recommend that candidates or applicants from the backward classes should be given proper coaching before enlistment and those who are on the borderland of average qualifications should be given further coaching even after selection, and thus, every effort should be made to train candidates from the backward classes to be efficient members of government services.

38. One paramount consideration that must be accepted is that just as efficiency and integrity are essential in government services, it is equally essential that the largest portion of the civil population should be trained to run the administraiton with integrity and efficiency. No democracy can be safe, if adequate qualification for government services is confined to a few communities only. Democracy, to be broad-based, must train the maximum number of citizens for the efficient discharge of public duties, especially in the case of a Welfare State, where the public sector is going to be increased by leaps and bounds, and the number of government services is being increased from day to day. It is essential that the government should have the maximum number of persons trained for running the administration from amongst all the communities.

39. We might even go to the length of recommending that the universities and institutions of secondary education should have specialised courses for training young men and young women for governmental administrative jobs. If mathematics, geography and similar subjects are essential, it is equally essential that principles of administration and the technique of running various departments of the government must also be compulsory subject in secondary and higher educational institutions.

40. Under a democracy, a government will be judged by the number of servants it is able to retain from all the communities composing the nation.

41. The Parliament could demand from the government an annual report showing how many candidates it trained in all in the art of administration.

Reservation in Institutes of Higher Education

42. As for assistance in the matter of education for the backward classes, I am convinced that introduciton of Basic Education in all the

States will help the backward communities to cultivate self-confidence. They will also have a better chance of succeeding in open competition, and having the special advantage of mixing with people and serving them, they will prove themselves better administrators and leaders of society.

43. Seats in the higher technical institutes of science, engineering, medicine, etc., will be limited for some years to come, and there should be a generous reservation in favour of the backward classes.

44. Here again, the best interests of the nation demand that the most intelligent and the most promising should be trained to supply the needs of the nation. You cannot deny the nation its right of being served by the best. In these days of keen competition, both in trade and war, no nation can afford to have indifferent persons trained to higher service. Here again, the fears of the backward classes that they will not be able to come up to the level of the upper classes are entirely unfounded. Students from the backward classes who have come up to matriculation standard can easily hold their own against the upper classes. Experience of the past is no guide for the achievements of the future. The backward classes are already feeling that they are the equals of the upper castes, and given a proper chance, they can easily hold their own.

45. But I am definitely of the opinion that in the field of education, the backward classes must be made to feel that here at least they will have everything in their favour, and that the nation is determined to give them the best chance of educating themselves and coming to the top. I have, therefore, whole-heartedly supported the recommendation that up to 70 per cent of the seats ought to be reserved for the best amongst the backward classes. The remaining 30 per cent seats, and any seats not absorbed by candidates from the 'Reserved' communities should go to the 'Unreserved' communities. This rule should apply for the next 10 years. It may be confined to all the existing institutes of higher technical education. The tension and the need for rationing will be eased as more institutes are opened. The nation is determined to develop in science and technology; so more and more institutes will be opened in the near future and almost everyone that has shown a capacity of succeeding in higher technical education, will get a seat. No reservation will then be necessary.

46. I would recommend that some institutes may be reserved specially for the benefit of the backward classes and the backward students could be admitted to these to the limit of 90 per cent, 10 per

cent being reserved for the upper communities, so that the students of the backward communities will have a chance of mixing freely and brushing their intellect against the intellect of students having more self-confidence. If this suggestion is followed, then institutes not reserved for the backward classes could throw their doors open to all students irrespective to communal considerations.

47. We have to hear the other side which also is important enough. Free India is struggling to come up to the level of the advanced nations of the world, not militarily but in education and material development, which will give best scope for the spiritual culture of India. The nation wants a highly trained personnel alike in scientific, technical and social fields. The nation is anxious to train all the backward classes to come up to the level of the advanced classes, but the nation may not be satisfied with the supply of highly trained personnel which is derived from the backward classes only. The hunger and thirst for men of the highest education and training are insatiable, and the nation may not deny itself the services of persons who could be trained from amongst the upper classes also. And, just as we are insistent that we shall have the services of the best pilots, best doctors and best engineers, to whatever class they may belong, the nation is equally anxious that it should train every person who has the potential capacity of responding to the training. We cannot therefore, prevent young men and young women from the advanced classes, from being trained to serve the nation humanity.

48. Social justice demands that the backward classes are not denied the chance of being similarly trained, but they cannot start with demanding a monopoly of 70 per cent of the chances of being trained for higher services.

49. If I have lent my full support to the demand for 70 per cent of reservations in higher technical institutes of learning for the backward classes it is not because I want to turn the upper classes into a new underprivileged class, but because I want opportunities for higher training to be multiplied with break-neck speed. It is only when the traditionally more promising sections of society are kept out of higher learning that those in authority and power will shed their traditional lethargy.

50. In the same spirit I once suggested that the Bhangis of a town living in filthy *bastis* should all be shifted *en bloc* to stay in college hostels; it is not that I did not want college education and amenities of residence for the students. I knew that only if all the college hostels

were requisitioned for the accommodation of the most useful servants of society, *viz*. the Bhangis, that society would bestir itself and make herculean efforts for having adequate housing accommodation for the students. Not mere agitation could drive the city fathers to build better quarters for the Bhangis.

51. In the same way, it is only when most of the available seats in institutions of higher learning are occupied by eligible candidates from the backward classes that the government and social leaders will come forward to start more and more institutions of technical education for training students denied admission into the higher institutes simply because they happen to belong to the upper and more promising communities.

The American Policy

52. Having thus given my viewpoint regarding reservations both in government service and in institutes of Higher Technical Education, I am tempted to give below the American policy of Fair Practice in Employment. America is a land of many races and nationalities. The Anglo-Saxons, the French, the Germans, the Latin races, the Jews, the Negroes, and the aboriginal Red-Indians, with a microscopic sprinking of a few Asians all thrown together, constitute a collossal problem which they are trying to solve in America. This is how they regulate employment under the merit system.

53. 'The long-established policy of the federal government, under the merit system of federal employment, has been to make appointments to federal positions will the sole regard to merit and fitness.'

54. 'This policy was reinforced in 1948, when President Truman issued Executive Order 9980 setting forth for the Federal Service the basic policy of fair employment without discrimination because of race, colour, religion or national origin. The fair employment policy does not mean that any fixed proportion of persons of different races, religions or national origins must be given Federal employment. It distinctly and definitely does not mean that any persons of interior merit or fitness shall be pushed ahead of other employees or applicants or shielded from the consequences of their failures or short-comings whether members of a majority group, or members of a minority group which in the past have suffered from an unfair discrimination. No applicant or employee having merit and fitness shall be refused or

deprived of employment or earned promotion by reason of his or her race, colour, religion, or national origin. On the same principle, no one lacking merit or fitness shall receive preferment for the same reasons. The fair employment policy is a double-edged tool and as such must be used with special care and good judgement.'

55. Some such policy will have to be followed by our country also when the unhappy but necessary period of reservations is over. We hope that by then, the various castes will have been amalgamated and there will also be free inter-marriages between various denominational groups. Not a mere co-existence of communities but National Solidarity is what we are aiming at.

Remedial Measures on Non-Caste Bases

56. According to the terms of reference to the Commission, we were asked to consider whether any sections of the people of the territory of India, in addition to the scheduled castes and scheduled tribes, should be treated as socially and educationally backward classes. The words specifically used are 'classes and sections' of the people, and not 'castes', and yet, as explained in the body of the report the word 'sections and classes' can in the present context mean nothing but castes, and no other interpretation is feasible.

57. It must be admitted, however, that, taking the wording of the terms of reference, we are not precluded from interpreting the words 'sections and classes of the people' in their widest significance even excluding the idea of caste. We feel we were justified in accepting the traditional interpretation. We were warned by well-wishers of the country that investigations into caste may encourage people to be caste-conscious, and thus increase the atmosphere of communalism. Following the analogy of the proverb, viz. 'using the thorn to remove a thorn,' we held that the evils of caste could be removed by measures which could be considered in terms of caste alone.

58. The result of our inquiry is that caste-consciousness, caste loyalties and caste aspirations, have increased throughout the country and some of us were responsible for encouraging people to think that the backward classes could be organised into a party to wield political power through universal adult franchise. (That position has been crystallised into my article 'Emergence of a New Leadership'. It expresses the hope and ambition of the backward classes, and it is also a warning to others regarding the atmosphere in the country and the

attitude which they must cultivate in order to meet the emergency.)

59. But, we cannot be oblivious to the dangers to the solidarity of the country. Communalism and casteism are bound to destroy the unity of the nation and narrow down the aspirations of our people.

60. Two years of experience have convinced us of the dangers of the spread of casteism and the warning of the well-wishers of the country have also led us, almost towards the end of our investigation, to the conclusion that it would have been better if we could determine the criteria of backwardness on principles other than caste.

61. We feel that the investigation into the backwardness in the nation and of the people ought not to have been confined to finding out such sections of the people or such classes, castes, communities or tribes as are backward. We have come to the conclusion that this group investigation is repugnant to the spirit of democracy.

62. In a democracy, it is always the individual (not even the family) which is the unit. Democracy thrives best when, on the one hand, we recognise and respect the personality of the totality comprising the nation.

63. Groups or sections, less than the totality of the nation, should not be encouraged to develop group loyalty as otherwise, the spirit of democracy is undermined.

64. Moreover, the nation has decided to establish a classless and casteless society, which also demands that backwardness should be studied from the point of view of the individual and, at the most, that of a family. Any other unit will lead to caste or class aggrandisement.

65. Let us, therefore, try to find criterion of backwardness that could eschew ideas of caste or class.

66. The following may be accepted as criteria of backwardness. It is a rough list and needs careful scrutiny, and yet these considerations are given below by way of guidance.

It would be more convenient to write the criterion in two columns showing the anti-thesis between the Backward and the Non-Backward.

Backward	*Non-Backward*
1. Women	1. Men
2. Residents of rural area	2. Residents of urban area
3. Those who are driven to the necessity of working with their own hands	3. Those whose work consists of supervision of manual workers

4. Those labouring under the sun and in open air	4. Those working under shade after the pattern of the white-collared fraternity
5. Landless labourers	5. Landed peasantry
6. Unskilled labour	6. Skilled labour and high craftsmanship
7. Not having sufficient, or any capital	7. Commanding sufficient capital
8. Working as mere clerks	8. Following some learned profession
9. Menial service under private persons	9. Government service of the upper grades
10. Having poor and uneducated parents, lacking ambition and having no vision	10. Having educated parents or guardians with an atmosphere of self-confidence and culture
11. Lacking in resources	11. Having adequate income and resources
12. Belonging to, or condemned to live in, inaccessible and backward areas	12. Enjoying amenities of modern civilisation
13. Illiterate	13. Having a fair amount of education
14. Not having capacity to understand modern times and the facilities for self-improvement available in society	14. Being well-equipped and alert to profit by modern conditions and opportunities
15. Belief in magic, superstition and fate	15. Belief in science and the understanding of the law of cause and effect

Remedies for Removing Backwardness

1. *Women*: They should be given special help in education so that they may come up to the level of men, and they should be given all opportunities in public service by giving them equality of status.

They should be given security of tenure in service during periods of pregnancy and childbirth.

2. *Rural areas*: Rural areas must be made attractive by better and

healthy amenities, etc. Educational institutions in sufficient numbers should be planted in rural areas, including a few rural universities.

3. *Working with hands*: All education should involve the use of hands and the cultivation of the use of fingers for scientific precision and artistic grace.

All work of a supervisory nature should be combined with some amount of manual labour in company of the regular manual workers.

Nobody should be allowed to be a boss unless he is prepared to do some manual work also.

4. *Working under the sun and in open air*: All amenities and comforts for those working in shade and those working under the sun should be equalised as much as possible, so that preference for 'shaded' life may automatically cease.

Difference in the emoluments or wages of the two should also be reduced to a minimum.

5. *Land*: Landless labourers should be given every facility of possessing some land, either individually or collectively, and nobody should be allowed to possess land unless he is prepared to hold the plough in his hand and work on the land for the major part of the year.

6. *Unskilled labour*: Special training should be given to the unskilled labourers to improve their efficiency, and they should be encouraged to raise the standard of efficiency, precision, dexterity grace and quickness. The unskilled labourers of today should also be allowed some leisure in which they could develop some kind of craftsmanship as a hobby.

All labour should be educated labour. The labouring men should be able to read and write, enjoy and understand the newspapers of the day. He must be encouraged to cultivate self-respect and ever increasing efficiency for himself and his children.

He should be given educational allowance for himself for some time, and afterwards, for his children.

7. *Capital*: Hereafter, there should be a ceiling on individual capital, all additional capital being socialised for the good of all.

8. *Clerkship and the learned professions*: Even mere administration should be regarded as a learned profession, along with that of the doctor, pleader, engineer and the educationist.

Clerks should be encouraged to help in evolving club-life, where they could improve their prospects by picking up new things by which they could add to their capacity and social utility.

9. *Menials, other grades and classes of service*: Employment of

menials must be discouraged. Everyone, whether high or low, should be expected to look after his own room, his office, his dress and the carrying of things from one place to another, etc.

The use of menial service should be confined to the needs of only the sick, the babies and the extremely old.

Heavy work, of course, will have to be tackled by collective effort.

There should also be collective service instead of personal menial service. For instance, instead of keeping a servant to do my marketing, I should ask the shop-keeper to maintain servants who would go to all the customers of the shop delivering things purchased by them.

Hours of work of the menial servants, the nurses, watchmen, waiters, etc., should be limited, and where employment is steady, there should be arrangement for regular promotion and pension after a period of service.

10. *Parentage*: There should be an army of social servants or social workers who would act in the place of parents for many children. This career should attract best men and best women. The State should be in the place of parents for looking after the youths of the land, giving them proper training and cultivating their ambition to be useful members of society.

11. *Resources*: The need for resources will be reduced to a minimum, if workshops and similar fields of work are socialised.

Till then the State should provide or lend or cheapen facilities.

12. *Inaccessible Areas*: The State should have a survey of all such areas, and hasten to have all-weather good *pucca* roads and approach roads as early as possible, and where population is sparse the people should be asked to given their quota of the expenses through manual labour, *i.e. Shramdan*, care being taken always never to build a *pucca* road unless it had with it the installation of the telephone also. This is essential for the safety of the traffic and for military needs also.

For mountainous areas there should be more of bridges of sufficient width for buses to ply.

13. *Literacy*: People should not wait for the government to start primary and basic schools. Social workers should enthusiastically start literacy campaign work. High school and college students should be encouraged, as part of their curriculum, to go to nearby villages, and spend a month or two of their vacation towards the spread of literacy. Special books should be published by the State, showing easy ways for the spread of literacy and general knowledge.

14. *Superstitious beliefs, etc.*: It is difficult to assess the

backwardness due to superstitious beliefs, but this kind of backwardness is spread over the whole world. This can be overcome by regular and systematic teaching of science and inductive logic. A sustained campaign against blind belief in magic, fate and superstitions, should be carried on. Much of caste predudices and race prejudices could be removed, and racial amity fostered by a systematic attack on superstitious beliefs and blind prejudices, religious or otherwise.

15. *Understanding of modern times and its amenities*: This is the crux of most of the backwardness amongst the masses. Systematic classes must be held throughout the country, and all the educational methods and psychological aids should utilised to enthuse, both social servants and the masses, for the spread of correct ideas about health, use of money, systems of administration, laws of psychology, sociology, ethics and spirituality.

Group prejudices and race prejudices should be analysed. Religious beliefs should be subjected to a close but sympathetic criticism of reason and logic. Latest instances of social prejudices should be analysed in detail and their hollowness exposed and then, people should be encouraged consciously to befriend those who are distant geographically, psychologically and culturally, thus leading to universal brotherhood and familyhood of all races.

Difficulties of the Next Census

67. We have recommended that the next census should give all the necessary information about castes and sub-castes. If would certainly be a valuable material for the sociologists and the anthropologists. Social reformers will profit by it. Demography the world over will be thankful if all this information is supplied. But a lurking suspicion is asserting itself in my mind: Can we do it?

68. A government can demand cooperation from its citizens and require the people to give certain information and statistics to the best of their knowledge, but can census officers force a citizen to give information which he is not prepared to volunteer? There is a growing body of citizens in India who refuse to accept caste, and who may refuse to tell or acknowledge the caste to which they happened to belong in the past.

69. Another question is: Can census authorities prevent a man from giving his caste according to his own concept? The *Sonar* (goldsmith)

in Maharashtra, for instance, may declare his caste simply as Brahman. The same *Sonar* in Assam may declare his caste as Harijan. A Brahman, recently, during our tour, declared that till yesterday he was Brahman, but now he elects to be a Harijan. If Mahatma Gandhi could do it why not I?', was his argument. There are many priests amongst the Harijans who have started calling themselves Brahmans. Who can prevent them from doring so? The great saint poet of Maharashtra, Sant Tukaram was a Bania by caste, but he always called himself a Shudra. Sardar Vallabhbhai Patel belonged to one of the dominant communities of Gujarat *viz.*, Patidars. There was a case in court, and the question was whether the Patidars should regarded as Kshatrias or Vaishyas. By occupation they are farmers. Leaders of the community came to Sardar Patel and requested him to give his evidence before the court. He said he had no objection, only he would tell the court that the Patidars are Shudras. Even a Brahman may elect to be a Shudra or a Harijan.

70. The next question is: Can a secular government force a citizen to belong or not to belong to a particular caste? A Brahman, if he becomes a Muslim or a Christian, can say that he is no longer a Brahman. Christianity and Islam will not than him if he persisted in giving his caste as Brahman even after conversion, and the State will have no option but to record his caste as he gives it. Now, it is necessary for a Hindu Brahman to renounce his Hinduism if he is keen on dropping his caste? And can the census clerks and enumerators put down the caste of a man according to their conception inspite of the protest of the person concerned? Is it not the duty of the enumerator honestly to note down whatever information is volunteered by the citizen without trying to consider whether the information volunteered is traditionally acceptable or not? At the last census, when a census man asked me about my religion, I told him that I belonged to all religions and I accepted all religions as mine. I do not know what he wrote actually in the census returns, but I think I have a right to prosecute him, if he puts down anything which I have not volunteered.

71. There are innumerable instances where poor and ignorant citizens do not now what answer to give to certain questions, and the enumerator writes down whatever suits his own predilection or fancy. I know of cases where some people gave Hindustani as their language, and the enumerator put it down as Hindi.

72. When caste becomes politically important and parties for elections are formed on the predilections of caste, census operations

will become as complicated as elections and the facts given may be challenged as not being above suspicion. I remember how, during a previous census in Assam, there was a complaint made by many people that the figures of Muslims were greatly inflated; and that is why the census returns, although ready and printed, were not published on the ground that the information may be misused by the enemy, it being war time.

73. Caste cannot stick to a man as his age, colour or sex. Caste, like religion, could be changed, as often as one likes, and there is no theocratic power in India left today which could regulate or challenge the professions of an individual. I do not think a secular State can insist on noting down the caste of a person. He may not own it and society may not recognise what the individual claimed.

74. Recently, some people belonging to the scheduled castes gave their caste name as Harijans. That was of course accepted, but then the State Government turned round and said that since the name Harijan is not to be found in the list of scheduled castes issued by the President of India, those who called themselves Harijans could not get the scholarships and concessions that were reserved for the scheduled castes!

75. Then there is further trouble during the last 50 years and more. People have started giving new, high-sounding, and what they regard as much more respectable names, to their own caste. The Chamar, for instance, may call himself Ravidas, that being the name of a saint who was born in that community. The barbers prefer to call themselves Sena. We can have no quarrel if such a change of name of a caste created no confusion. But, take the instance of the great sage Valmiki. People say that he was originally a Brahman, but he became a fisherman, and joined the ranks of the highway men and started murdering and looting wayfarers. Now, any Brahman can easily take Valmiki as his surname. The fishermen can call themselves Valmiki, and so can the ex-criminal tribes people. Today, some of the scavenging castes also call themselves Valmiki. Now, what are the census authorities to do? And, what is the department of education also to do?

76. English spelling and typographical mistakes also have created a number of castes, which also has led to strange confusion. Dasa is a community amongst the Shudra. Dasa means a servant or a slave. Pious people use the suffix Dasa when they accept some name of the diety as their own. Even men of the upper castes thus, call themselves

Dasa. Purushottamdas, Purandaradas, Prabhudas, are instances is point. And, as irony would have it, some of the Jains were divided into two groups of 10 families and 20 familes, popularly known as Dasa and Visa meaning 10 and 20 respectively. Now, Dasa meaning 10 was also spelt as DASA. So, the Dasa amongst the Jains, a flourishing mercantile community, were confused with the Shudra community. Dasa. Such difficulties could, of course, be obviated by using the *Nagri* spelling of words, but it is not easy for the next census to secure detailed and accurate figures and information about castes.

77. The problem of caste and religion is bound to be further complicated by the ever-growing number of inter-marriages between persons of different castes and different religions.

78. What shall be the recognised caste of persons so marrying, and that of their progeny? The old simple rule was that the wife necessarily took the caste and religion of the husband and the children also did the same. But men marrying wives from lower castes were often times outcasted and were relegated to the status of a lower caste.

79. The Roman Catholics say that if any of their girls married a non-Christian, they would not object provided that children of such union were brought up as Catholics. Sometimes the marrying couple do not wish to disturb each other's caste or religion and the children are left to choose their religion for themselves. And we shall soon have a body of citizens who will declare that they belong to no caste and no religion.

80. It will be equally difficult to ascertain the different names–old and new–of the same caste and sub-caste. Propagandists will be active in persuading people to chose particular names and formulae.

81. It is already being proposed that people going in for mixed marriages should claim to belong to the lowest class and there is no authority in the land, universally recognised, that can regulate the caste of people hereafter.

82. Thus the confusion and anarchy of opinion about all communal matters is going to make the work of the next census well-nigh impossible.

Dominant Communities

83. The history of the past 100 years shows that in the beginning one or two upper communities claimed that they represented the whole nation and they stood for the best interests of the people. This claim was

92. But it is not easy to guarantee that representatives of the dominant communities will not tyrannise over the scheduled castes, the scheduled tribes and the starred communities. Tyrants and bullies cannot be made into protectors of the people by being put at the head of the backward classes.

93. The spirit of domination is a vice and a curse. It is a disease that is spread over the whole world. There are dominant races who victimise others. The European nations have shown that they could do when they got the chance of spreading over the whole world. Priests of old have dominated an ignorant and superstitious humanity. In India today, there are dominant communities even amongst the untouchables. In Maharashtra we heard the complaint that the Mahars amongst the untouchables dominated all the rest. In northern India a similar complaint was levelled against the Chamars. In the extreme south the Ezhavas and Nadars are said to dominate other scheduled castes.

94. It can safely be said that those who possess large tracts of land, those who have money enough to lend, those who have brains to create quarrels and factions amongst the people, and those who have the tradition of wielding governmental power, are all dominant people in rural areas. Northern India has given us the formula of AJGAR, a word formed by taking the initial letters of the four communities — *A*hir, *J*at, *G*ujjar and *R*ajput (AJGAR means the Boa-constrictor, that quietly swallows and leisurely digests many animals. Such Ajgar communities are to be found in both the upper and the lower castes. In Sind, the Amils dominated all the rest, whether Hindus or Muslims. In Gujarat, it was the Nagar, the Patidar and the Anavil who are said to have dominated all the rest; and some times, the Patanwadias or Padhiars have retaliated in desperation. In Maharashtra, besides the Brahman it is the Maratha who claimed to be the ruling community in the villages, and the Prabhu, that dominated all other communities. In Karnataka the Lingayat and the Vokkaliga, in Andhra the Kamma and the Reddy, in Tamil Nadu the Mudaliar and the Naidu, in Kerala, the Nair and the Ezhava, in Bengal the Kayastha and the Baidya, in Assam, the Ahom, in Bihar the Rajput and the Bhumihar, in Orissa, the Khandayat and Karnam, etc., are declared to be dominant — the list is neither exhaustive nor authoritative. Some of these communities might have been accused by mistake or by prejudice, but the fact remains that there are certain communities that are dominant. The pehnomenon obtains throughout the world and it is the special mission of the present age to give courage to victim communities to resist all tyranny. In

England the mercantile community successfully resisted the domination fo the feudal Barons during the Industrial Revolution and, recently, labour is successfully resisting the domination of both.

95. It is, therefore, essential that no dominating community should be allowed to claim to be the protector of the weaker sections. It is only the good men from every community, men who are imbued with a sense of social justice, who can forget caste prejudice, are prepared to surrender their privileges and who can combine to usher is a new era of social justice and universal familyhood, that can be the natural leaders and protectors of the helpless, mute and suffering masses.

96. We have to recognise that there are certain communities who are financially well off and, yet, are educationally backward, and a good many of them have been dominating society, especially of the rural areas. In the religions or orthodox hierarchy, they may not belong to the upper castes, but by their wealth and prestige, they are dominant. Sometimes they possess vast acres of land; sometimes they have amassed sufficient capital to work as money-lenders. These landlords and money-lenders dominate the whole village scene. Upper castes like the Brahamans and the Banias have to bend before the will of these dominant communities. Even government servants have to respect their wishes. Government servants are often times coaxed, cajoled, bribed, and so made to connive at the traditional domination and bullying of these against the low and subservient classes.

97. I consented to include in the backward classes list such dominant communities who, although not socially backward, could be regarded so because of their having neglected education. I had hoped that I could classify them into a separate sub-head and help them fight successfully the privileges of the upper communities.

98. I wanted so to classify the backward clases that the dominant communities amongst the officially backward could successfully put up a fight against the upper castes and, yet, become impotent to tyrannise over the weaker sections amongst the backward.

99. I did not succeed in this effort because I could not carry conviction to my colleagues that these dominant communities must be segregated if the victims of domination have to be saved.

Political Leadership

100. In my own province of Maharashtra, new political and social life began with able leaders like Justice Ranade, Telang, Prof. Bhandarkar,

the Hon'ble Gokhale, and Lokamanya Tilak. They started an allround movement of political, social, religious and industrial reform and regeneration. They naturally and justifiably claimed to represent the whole nation. They got full cooperation from noble persons like Dadabhoy Nowrojee, Sir Pherozeshah Mehta, Badruddin Tyabji, Barrister Baptista and others.

101. But a movement soon started, called the non-Brahman movement, headed by some leaders of the Maratha community, like the Raja of Kolhapr. This movement was, to some extent, anti-Congress and pro-British. They also got full support from good many Muslims, Christians and others. The leaders of the non-Brahman movement asserted that the so-called leaders of the Congress were chiefly Brahmans and therefore, communal. Whereas they themselves represented the whole nation.

102. This movement travelled south and there also, the non-Brahman movement included the Muslims and the Christians. They claimed to represent the whole nation. But unfortunately, they fought shy of the nationalist movement led by the Congress.

103. With the advent of Mahatma Gandhi and Sardar Vallabhbhai Patel, in the political field the situation changed. The non-Brahman following discovered where their real interest lay. They saw that Mahatma Gandhi and Vallabhabhai Patel were non-Brahmans, and yet, they could lead the Congress and work for the betterment of the masses. And all classes worked under them. The Brahmans were the first to join their forces.

104. Orthodox leaders of the old non-Brahman movement basked in the sunshine of governmental favours, and a few families of some of the leading communities advanced considerably. There was a general awakening in the masses to rise educationally and also socially. There were caste conferences everywhere in the country. The general trend of these conferences was to collect funds for instituting scholarships for children of their own communities. They ransacked ancient history, real or fanciful, to upgrade themselves and traced their descent from some Brahman or Kshatriya *rishi* or king of old. They also asked the Census Department to help them in collecting caste-wise figures to ascertian the strength of their population.

105. With the growth of political life and spread of education many communities from amongst the non-Brahmans became advanced enough (although in Mysore, today, the government recognises only the Brahmans as the advanced community and all others are officially

backward, although the prominent amongst these backward communities have monopolised all political power. It is they who manage the universities also. They dominate the learned professions and trade. The Brahmans, although they have not been driven to the wall, have consented to occuy the second place). In northern India, as also in southern India, now, the position is that about half a dozen or a dozen communities are bracketed with the Brahmans. They are the leaders of today. They are now declared, of course, justifiably, to be the advanced communities.

106. Their leadership of the whole nation is now being sought to be challenged.

107. It is now the turn of the dominant (and sometimes bullying) communities and individuals amongst the backward classes to claim to be the leaders of the bulk of the nation. As yet they are not claiming to be the leaders of the whole nation. With communistic ideas they could certainly do so, but today, they exclude the advanced communities from amongst them and they regard themselves to be the leaders of all the backward communities. They resent the backward communities being classified into:

(i) slightly backward;
(ii) more backward; and
(iii) those who are leading a sub-human existence (We have put a star before such communities in our list).

They say that this would create a division in their ranks. They want all the backward classes to be organised in a solid phalanx against the advanced commmunities and even the most nationalistic and least communal from among the advanced communities are not allowed the right to speak for, or represent the backward communities. They are allowed to serve the backward classes no doubt, but they must do so under the guidance and leadership of these dominant amongst the backward.

108. If public life is thus allowed to be developed into a struggle between rival factions, national solidarity and strength will be weakened. The dominant amongst the backward hope to capture power and rule over the whole country. There is nothing wrong in this ambition provided they do not pit the backward classes against the advanced communities and create a conflict. Let them accept the unity and homogeneity of the nation and train themselves to lead the whole

nation. Such leadership is already theirs if they can serve the whole nation including the backward classes loyally and not imitate the selfish among the upper classes in aggrandising themselves on the strength of the numbers of the blind following of the extremely backward they can always count upon the cooperation of the best amongst the advanced classes. If they do not follow such wise policy, all administration, public life, industries, commerce, etc., may be jeopardised, and then the extremely backward will discover that they have been duped. This will give rise to a revolt from the bottom which will ultimatley end in chaos.

109. I have painted this dismal picture, not as a prophet but simply as a warning to all concerned. The advanced communities, especially, should recognise the signs of the times and shed their sense of superiority and aloofness, and monopolistic tendency. They should befriend one and all without any distinction. They should encourage inter-caste marriages at all levels. If no social conflict is contemplated and the Sarvodaya ideal of working for the upliftment of all beginning with the lowest of the low, is the source of inspiration, then it is immaterial to whose hands the leadership is transferred. It is much better, if new communities are allowed to try their hand at leadership. Only those who, like Nehru, are above communal considerations and even nationalistic considerations, should be allowed to formulate the policy of the nation. It is no use challenging the leadership of the best in the land by searching out the community to which they belong, and then accusing them that they are monopolising leadership for the upper classes. All monopoly must be broken even if it is fully justified and opportunities for service must be assured to all sections of the population.

Ministry of A.B.C.

110. One important unanimous recommendation of ours is regarding the formation of a separate Ministry for the amelioration of the conditon of all the backward classes.

111. The problem of backwardness is not merely one of serving a few minorities here and there, but it is a problem of the reconstruction of society itself. It is a changeover from the medieval feudal basis to a modern democratic society based on equal respect for the personality of every individual. Far-reaching changes in human relations are necessary. If our recommendation in this regard, is accepted, the

government will have to find for this ministry a statcman of the first rank, having widest sympathy, tact, courage and vision. Someone of the calibre of Shri Dhebar alone can do justice to this task of effecting a social revolution, envisaged in our report.

112. The *Panchkroshi* schools for the initiation of a novel type of Rural Basic Education will tax the genius of a ture educationist.

113. The *Samata Ashrams*, recommended in the Report, will, it is hoped, herald the beginning of Sarvodaya Society.

114. The revival of village industries and handicrafts, on a nation-wide cooperative basis, will instil new life into the masses.

115. The artisan, when rehabilitated, will reflect the culture of a non-violent, rural civllisation.

116. The whole movement for the liquidation of all backwardness will have to be lifted from the level of mere job-hunting and the impotent resentment at being frustrated in this pursuit.

An Explanation

117. I have always held that universal adult franchise is the best panacea against many social and political ills from which the masses suffer. The adult franchise assures even the meanest of the citizens that he has a stake in the country and that he is being governed with his own consent. I am proud that the Constituent Assembly accepted Mahatmaji's suggestion and incorporated universal adult franchise as a cardinal principle of our Constitution. By this franchise all power is already transferred to the masses. If they are not today able to wield this power, it is becausse they lack education and wise political guidance. I have always said that giving an additional weapon in weak hands is no remedy. I am defnitely against giving special political representation or powers to anybody, over and above the universal adult franchise.

118. Some representatives of the backward classes complained that the representatives do not realy represent their case because the masses do not know how to choose their representatives. I told them that their plea amounted to a suggestion that the masses do not deserve to have the vote, and, therefore, it should be taken away from them.

119. This has been interpreted by certain interested persons to mean that I am against the backward classes being given any political power. It is no use answering each and every misrepresentation. A thing which has no substance in truth can safely be allowed to die a natural death. I

know it is not going to harm me even temporarily because I am seeking no political power or leadership. I am also accused of saying that the masses might sell their country to India's enemies. The masses, as a whole, have never been known to sell their country, and if they did, nothing on earth can prevent them from doing so. It is generally the unscrupulous opportunists who claim to represent the people that are likely to sell their country, and this ignoble characteristic is not the monopoly of either the upper classes or the lower classes. People have been found here and their, since ancient times, to be traitors to their country. The only remedy lies in building a strong democracy, and cultivating a high standard of political morals. Often times, people sell their country through lack of political wisdom and shrewd ability to detect the wiles of the country's enemies. The remedy against this danger also is political maturity which comes only through wielding of political power by the masses.

120. In the final analysis, I stand for a social order in which neither religion nor political power are organised to control the destinies of humanity. Just as we stand for a secular democracy, I stand for a non-political social order based on mutual love, trust, respect and service. But, this has nothing to do with the universal adult franchise which I accept whole-heartedly.

121. Some people might say that our Report reads more like a manifesto on behalf of the backward classes than a document giving the views of all sections of people and arriving at a considered and balanced decision by the Commission, I admit that the Report could have been written in a different way, but we thought it better to put it in the way we did, because we wanted to support our conclusions by mentioning the feelings and grievances of the backward classes. It is they who are neglected and not the upper classes. There is another reason. The upper classes, either out of apathy or out of generosity for the backward classes, did not care to come out with their views before the Commission. They perhaps thought that this was another enquiry on behalf of another minority, and they had no objection if some provision was made for these people also. In fact, many people even in responsible positions believed, and still believe, that the Commission was out to inquire into the condition of the Harijans and the Girijans. Many people, highly placed in government and in public life, repeated this misconception to our great astonishment and regret. It was to warn such people that I was driven to broadcast an article about 'The Emergence of a New Leadership'. Even this article was noticed,

mainly by the represntatives of the backward classes. This article was followed by a radio talk in which I pleaded for an atmosphere of brotherly cooperation and not one of antagonism and social conflict.

122. Towards the end of our inquiry, we have come to the conclusion that caste, communal or denominational considerations need not be introduced in the educational policy. A progressive, modern welfare State cannot afford to tolerate educational backwardness anywhere in the State. In most of the modern States, more than 60 per cent of the scholars receive full educational aid. In India, it should be possible for the State to give educational aid to all the poor and deserving students in the country, irrespective of caste, sex or denomination. Whenever it is necessary to show perference it must be for women and for students of rural areas. The present preference for the scheduled castes and scheduled tribes should be continued for some time, but the time has come when all the poor and deserving should, and could, be helped, so that no communal consideration need be introduced in the field of education.

123. It will be recognised that the Report gives expression both to the fears and aspirations that have no bearing for the future. It is but natural that backward people should think of their woes of the past. Very few people have the Gift of realising the gathering forces of tomorrow and those that suffered in the past cannot easily begin to believe in any glowing picture of the future. It is not by criticising them for their narrowness of outlook, but by introducing them as honoured members of the nation. To the benefits of the glorious future we are building, that they will shed their fears of the past and only them that the narrow and pigmy aspirations which they had *hugged* to their bosom will give place to a new and brighter hope.

124. Lastly, it is my pleasant duty to thank all those who contributed to the success of our labours.

125. To begin with, I must thank the various co-opted members who, even at the shortest notice, consented to tour with the Commission in their respective States and helped us with their local knowledge.

126. I must also thank the various public leaders and representatives of the various institutions serving the backward classes. Some of them were extremely frank and made us ponder over the many and conflicting sides of the problem.

127. The officers who were deputed by the State Governments to accompany the Commission were uniformly helpful and obliging and

128. We were able to discuss freely and frankly with the Ministers of the various States. We are grateful for the courtesy shown to us by them.

129. I must here express my personal and heartfelt gratitude to all my colleagues for their wonderful cooperation and consideration. They were kind enough to put up with my many shortcomings and irregularities.

130. The whole work of the office was shouldered by the Member-Secretary, Shri Arunangshu De, thus sparing my time for the main task.

131. The official secretaries from Shri Raman to Shri Nagar helped us with their intimate knowledge of governmental machinery and its procedure.

132. Everything depended on the willing, able and enthusiastic cooperartion of the section officers. I must thank the government for selecting Shri Gupta and Shri Sareen for our work. They displayed tact and understanding at every step, and with their own hard work, inculcated the same spirit in the staff.

133. The Research Section was started as my special hobby, but it soon developed into an important section. The Research Officers worked as hard as the rest of the staff, collecting and collating valuable material.

134. Shri S.K. Murthy worked as my Private Secretary. He worked diligently throughout the two years of the Commission's work. He could be trusted with any confidential work.

135. I must not forget the silent and devoted service of the office staff down to the peons who often times had to work hard beyond office hours. My heart goes out to them in their domestic joys and anxieties.

136. I must express my special obligation to Shri Datar (the Deputy Minister for Home Affairs) and Shri Laxmidas Shrikant (Commissioner for scheduled castes and scheduled tribes) for taking a keen personal interest in our work.

137. And most of all I am grateful to you, Rashtrapatiji, for giving us this valuable opportunity of studying the condition of a neglected and yet most lovable section of our nation and of serving them through this inquiry.

Yours sincerely,
KAKA KALELKAR
Chairman
Backward Classes Commission

POST SCRIPT

The Handloom Weaver and the Ambar Yarn

We have unanimously come to the conclusion that for the economic, educational and cultural rehabilitation of one of the biggest backward classes in India, it is essential that the village textile industry should be revived. We have unanimously recommended that first preference should be given to the Khadi industry and nothing should be done that may come in the way of the full and speedy development of Khadi. But the present limitations of our resources have set a limit to the production of Khadi in India. The remaining non-Khadi sector of textiles should, therefore, be reserved for the handloom, to the exclusion of mill or foreign cloth. We have recommended, in effect, that mill cloth should be prohibited from competing either with Khadi or handloom cloth. The mills may be helped to export their products to neighbouring countries.

2. In this connection, we have recommended that wherever Khadi is not able to occupy a field, government should arrange for the adequate supply of mill yarn, both coloured and uncoloured at reasonable rates to the handloom weavers. We also recommended that State Governments may start spinning mills to ensure such regular supply of yarn.

3. But a new and efficient instrument of production of yarn has recently been developed. It is known as *Ambar Charkha*. The strength, eveness and durability of yarn from this *Charkha* is in no way inferior to the mill yarn. Ambar yarn is definitely and decidedly superior in strength and evenness to hand-spun yarn. The *Ambar Charkha* is practically a domestic mill, for the production of good yarn.

4. I am certain that my colleagues would not have objected to the following proposal if it was placed before them, at the time of finalising our Report. I knew about the *Ambar Charkha*, but was not confident that it could be recommended as a practical proposition for the full supply of yarn that is necessary to make all the handlooms work, but my recent visit to the Sarvodaya Sammelan at Puri, and my detailed discussions with people that know, has emboldened me to make the following proposals:

> Government should manage to produce *Ambar Charkhas* in large numbers and supply them to the villages, government can also arrange to work the *Ambar Charkhas* with electric power and

thereby supply quality yarn to the handloom.

It has been found that even those weavers who find it difficult to weave hand-spun yarn, have no difficulty in utilising the Ambar Yarn.

The production of Ambar yarn is tantamount to decentralising the spinning mill industry with little capital, and the employment of more people than the mill industry can assure. I, therefore, recommend that next to the protection, given to Khadi, the State Government would do well to employ all handlooms for the production both of the utility cloth and artistic cloth, with the help of the Ambar yarn.

Christians and Non-Christian Tribals

5. During our tours of various States, we heard bitter complaints from non-Christian tribals that owning to the peculiar policy of the government they did not get all the advantages which they ought to get and which the Christian tribals generally get in abundance.

6. They said that 'during British rule, Christian Missionaries had a privileged position. Indian social servants were prevented from going into the excluded areas where the tribals lived. The Missionaries had the full monopoly there. Consequently the Christian tribals got better education in English; naturally they got into government service and generally their position was greatly improved. We knew that under British rule, it could not be otherwise.

> 'But even after the advent of 'Swaraj', conditions have not changed. Most of the concessions given by the Swaraj Government towards the betterment of the tribals go to the Christian tribals. The Christian Missions have now better facilities of proselytisation and the number of Missionaries in the midst of the tribals has increased. Even in the matter of political representation, it is the Christian tribals that generally manage to get our votes and they claim to represent the whole of the tribal population with the result that there is a political pressure put on non-Christian tribals to accept Christianity. We are *surprised* that even under Swaraj we are not safe in our devotion to our own religion'.

7. This complaint of the non-Christian tribals has quite a different complexion from usual complaint of ordinary Hindus against the proselytisation work of the Christian Missionaries. Hindus are

politically conscious enough to understand a policy of being extra fair to and placating the Christians in order to overcome the narrow prejudices of Hindus against non-Hindus; but the tribals cannot be expected to relish such differential treatment and what they regard as partially against them and in favour of Christian tribals.

8. We have, therefore, to consider the following points:

(i) Christians and Muslims are not satisfied with being treated indifferently as Indian citizens. They want special consideration and recognition for themselves. The Hindus are not allowed to say 'treat all Indian citizens as one, and don't divide us into Hindus and non-Hindus'. But when it comes to the position of tribals, division of the tribals into Christian tribals and non-Christian tribals is not favoured. Any such attempt is wounding the solidarity of the Christian tribals with the non-Christian triabls. The result is that Christian tribals being better educated and better organised have an opportunity of claiming to be the leaders of all the tribals. In a population of nearly two crores of tribals, the Christian tribals are only four lakhs and yet they are allowed to be the leaders of the two crores.

No body is against the help given to the Christian tribals. Let them be given better posts in government services because of their advancement; let them be treated with whatever special consideration the government finds it necessary. But why should they be allowed to be the leaders of all the non-Christian tribals and why should the non-Christian tribals be left to be the victims of the policy of domination of the Christian tribals.

(ii) The English language continues to be the medium of administration even after the advent of Swaraj, with the result that those who know English form an upper caste and have a better chance of getting government services especially in the upper grades. So far as Hindus and Muslims are concerned, this situation may wound their national pride but it does not wound their prospects; but with the tribals, so long as English is a medium of administration, only Christian tribals will prosper under Swaraj Government and non-Christians will not be able to raise their head for many generations to come. Even in Jamshedpur the Christian tribals are in the ascendant. They get all the upper employments in the Tata Factories because they are English educated.

(iii) As the Anthropologists love to dèclare, the tribals are animists. Hinduism has never disowned animistic groups. Hinduism is broad enough to accept the whole gamut of religious progress from extreme fetishism and animism to the highest fights of the Vedanta, and Indian culture from the earliest times has always accepted the tribals as part and parcel of the Hindu fold. It is cruel, therefore, to regard the tribals as non-Hindus. But perhaps the propaganda of British officers and Christian Missionaries has succeeded and some of the tribals are calling themselves non-Hindus. It is surprising that even the Swaraj Government is equally fond of dividing the tribals into animists and Hinduised tribals. Only Christian tribals are not separated from non-Christians.

9. The Christian Missionaries pressed upon the government to recognise ordinary Christians as a distinct community from the Hindus and they say this distinction must be observed because the Christians are in a minority. Then why not classify the tribals into Christian tribals and non-Christian tribals?

10. The Muslims and the Christians are minorities. Any special consideration shown to them is not going to endanger the solidarity of the Indian nation. It will be strengthened. Let Christian tribals be given every facility for their betterment, but let not the non-Christian tribals be put under the domination of the Christian tribals.

11. The very purpose of the Backward Classes Commission is to help the under-dog to save himself from the domination of the upper-dog. But here in the case of the tribals, we are allowing the non-Christian tribals to be dominated by the Christian tribals.

12. We are not anxious to curtail honest proselytising activities of the Christians although the Christians say that it is their religious duty and political right to go about asking all non-Christians to drop their own religion and accept Christianity. But it is one thing to permit the Christian Missionaries to preach their religion without any let or hindrance, but it is another thing to give help to the proselytising agencies through the tax payers' money, to dominate the non-Christian tribals.

KAKA KALEKAR
Chairman

POST SCRIPT 2

Sindhi Refugees

I am sorry, in the stress of various discussions, I entirely forgot to add a Chapter on Sindhi Refugees in my forwarding note. I do it now and hope that the following will kindly be incorporated in it.

I know the government is alive to the difficulties of Sindhis and is doing its best to relieve their sufferings but there are some of their difficulties which could be removed only by pursuing a policy which the Backward Classes Commission could recommend with propriety.

The Sindhi Hindus are an energetic and resourceful community. The way they have met the calamity has evoked admiration from all, but their woes are many. I would suggest, therefore, that all the Sindhi refugees should be regarded temporarily, i.e. for the next seven years, as a backward community and they should be given all the facilities, especially in the matter of scholarships for education, and priority in government service. One thing that specially came under our notice is that although some of them may not need any financial assistance, their children need the same special facilities for admission into institutes of higher and technical learning as are accorded to the members of backward communities. Sindhis had to leave their hearths and homes and they were forced to spread out and settle down in distant parts of the country. They had to suffer from the difficulty of language and oftentimes there was none who could sponsor their cause. Given proper facilities for admission into institutes of higher learning, Sindhis would make the best use of this concession and within a few years cease to be a dependent community.

Sindhi girls need special assistance and protection. I need not go into the details of this, but I hope the government will understand the need of the situation and declare the Sindhi refugees especially their women as a temporarily backward community for the next seven years.

KAKA KALEKAR
Chairman

CHAPTER SEVEN

The Kaka Kalelkar Commission Recommendations

The present chapter reproduces the conclusions, suggestions and recommendations made by the First Backward Classes Commission chaired by Kaka Kalelkar.

Report of the (First) Backward Classes Commission (1953-56)
(Chairman: Kaka Kalelkar)

SUMMARY OF CONCLUSIONS AND RECOMMENDATIONS

1. Census and Caste

Before the disease of caste is destroyed all facts about it have to be noted and classified in a scientific manner as in a clinical record. To this end we suggest that the 1961 Census be remodelled and reorganised so as to secure the required information on the following lines:

1. The Census operation should be conducted as a well-equipped continuous organisation competent to supply information on various topics of sociological importance.
2. The Census Offices must have permanent ethnologists and sociologists in addition to the economists attached to them.
3. As long as social welfare and social relief have to be administered through castes, classes or groups, full information about these groups should be obtained and tabulated.
4. Some of the staff for the census should be recruited from social workers and village-level workers of the Planning and Development Departments.

5. Estimated family income and expenditure should be collected and tabulated.
6. The Census slips should consist amongst others 'caste' in a separate column. If possible, Census should be carried out in 1957 instead of in 1961.

2. Special Groups

1. *Muslims*: It would not be correct or just to list all Muslims as socially and educationally backward. But there are a number of communities amongst them that are suffering from social inferiority in their own society and consequent educational backwardness. Such backward communities are included in the list of other backward classes. Various State governments have mentioned such communities under separate heads of Hindu and Muslim backward communities. But the Commission has indicated the names of the communities to include those of Muslims and Hindus.
2. *Christians:* Christianity has consistently refused to recognise caste. And yet, in practice, it was found that segregation of converts from the scheduled castes was not successfully overcome in certain parts of South India. We have included such communities, especially in the South, in the list of other backward classes. We add that if scheduled caste converts to Christianity in other parts of the country also suffer from any recognisable degree of segregation and social disability their case should be considered for being included in the list of other backward classes.
3. *Anglo-Indians*: The problem of Anglo-Indians does not come strictly within the purview of our inquiry. Yet, certain representations were made on their behalf. The Constitution of India guaranteed certain concessions to this community for a fixed period. Apart from this, this community cannot be classed as backward either educationally or socially.
4. *Eurasians in Travancore-Cochin*: A small community in the extreme south which is really Eurasian in character is now being called Anglo-Indians in the list published by the Education Ministry, Government of India. This nomenclature is a mistake. It may be renamed Eurasian for the purpose of relief and included in the list of other backward classes of Travancore-Cochin State.

5. *Sikhs:* It is our view that the Sikhs constitute an integral part of the broader Hindu religion. Although, in theory, the Sikhs do not subscribe to caste system, in actual practice they cling to many Hindu traditions and practices. We recommend that the communities or groups who are treated as untouchables among the Sikhs should be included in the list of scheduled castes. Any distinct community among the Sikhs found to be socially and educationally backward must be included in the list of other backward classes.
6. *Gurkhas*: The Gurkhas are socially and culturally an integral part of the Hindu community. Such of the communities among the Gurkhas found in Uttar Pradesh, Bihar and West Bengal, who are educationally and socially backward, are included in the list of other backward classes. In the rest of India they are known to ignore caste and to live as one homogeneous community. Such of those who have settled down in other States (except U.P., Bihar and West Bengal) should be included in the iist of other backward classes if they are found to be socially and educationally backward.
7. *Bhangis:* The lot of Bhangis at present is far from satisfactory. Their living conditions are bad and the tools with which they work should enable them to carry out their work in a more decent and hygienic manner. The Bhangis should not be condemned to live in segregated locations. They should be distributed and given quarters among other groups.
8. *Women*: Women in India have lived under great social handicaps and as a class must be regarded as backward. But since they do not form a separate community they cannot be included in the list of backward classes. The condition of women among the backward classes is worse. The girls from among the backward classes should be given better facilities for education. They should be encouraged to live in special hostels for girls of all communities. They should be trained in basic education. Women should have a share in the political life of the country.

   The following measures are recommended for the advancement of women in general:

   (i) Free education in all stages to all girls whose parents' income is less than Rs. 3,000 per annum.
   (ii) Scholarships for girls belonging to the backward classes.

(iii) Residential hostels for girl students, with priority for girls of the backward classes.

(iv) *Samata Ashrams* for girls of all communities to be run by trained staffs of women and men.

(v) Creation of special facilities for girls to study Medicine, Home Science, and other subjects specially suited for women.

(vi) More facilities for training women in the Fine Arts, and in Social Service.

9. *Unfortunate Women:* The administration of the 'Suppression of Immoral Traffic Act' is found to be more punitive than reformative. It is found that the punished offenders drift back to their old profession in the absence of any properly organised rescue homes where they could find refuge. There is great scope for starting rescue homes and the government should be able to help such efforts with finance and legislation. Rescue homes should not be mere asylums for such women. Such homes must be controlled by committees consisting of social workers under government supervision. Women social workers from well-to-do society should accept an increasingly larger role in tackling this problem. In addition to providing food and shelter for these unfortunate women, they must be taught different occupations to enable them to earn a living and become useful members of society. They must also be taught to change their outlook and to lead normal married lives.

10. *Delinquent Children:* The lower sections of society often neglect their children with the result that the latter go astray and sometimes become the victims of greed, cupidity and passion. Such children generally learn all kinds of vices and are trained to deceit and crime. The provisions for the rehabilitation of delinquent children are totally inadequate. It is not legislation that matters but better provision for the maintenance and education of such children that counts; it is the quality of the reforming agency that is all-important. The State must help persons who take up the work of amelioration of these delinquent children.

11. *Denotified Communities (Ex-Criminal Tribes):* The following measures are recommended for adoption for the amelioration of the conditions of the communities in this group:

(i) The Ex-Criminal Tribes should hereafter be called denotified communities. (*Vimochit Jatian*).

(ii) These communities have been classed as scheduled castes, scheduled tribes or other backward classes according to the criterion applicable to them for the purpose of relief.

(iii) The nomadic groups should be given facilities for leading a settled life. Efforts must be made to distribute them in the towns and villages so that they could gradually be assimilated by society.

(iv) The children of these groups should be trained in Basic Education. They must also be trained in cottage industries, handicrafts and agriculture. Services of trained psychologists and social workers should be employed to reform these habitual offenders.

(v) Group criminality should be treated differently from the acquired criminality of the individuals.

12. *Backward Areas:* Backward areas in Himachal Pradesh, Uttar Pradesh, Udaipur in Rajasthan, Bastar in Madhya Pradesh, Alirapur and Jobat in Madhya Bharat, Amarakantak in Vindhya Pradesh should be developed by allocating more community projects, National Extension Service blocs, Social Welfare Extension projects and other developmental schemes. The proposals of some of the States to declare them as Scheduled Areas may be examined by the Government of India and early action taken.

Criteria of Backwardness

A variety of causes – social, environmental, economic and political – have operated both openly and in a subtle form for centuries to create the present colossal problem of backwardness. Economic backwardness is the result and not the cause of many social evils of the present day. Social backwardness, therefore, is not today due to the particular profession of a person. It is not easy to group sections of people under certain occupations. There are certain distinct communities who are not confined to any one occupation and it would be difficult to categorise them under any known occupation. There are certain castes and sub-castes based on regionalism.

The Commission is justified in interpreting the terms of reference as mainly relating to social hierarchy based on caste. Caste generally depends upon birth; it may also depend upon habits and it may create further cleavage due to conventions and denominational differences.

After a consideration of the social conditions in Indian society and the causes for backwardness of a large section of the people, the following criteria are adopted for general guidance:

(i) Low social position, in the traditional caste hierarchy of Hindu society.
(ii) Lack of general educational advancement among the major section of a caste or community.
(iii) Inadequate or no representation in government service.
(iv) Inadequate representation in the field of trade, commerce and industry.

Classification of Communities

We have taken into consideration the social position which a community occupies in the social hierarchy, the percentages of literacy and its general educational advancement; and its representation in government service or in the industrial sphere. The economic backwardness had also to be kept in view in order to find out the ability of the community to take advantage of the available opprtunities as also the recent trends in its advancement.

The list of other backward classes published by the Education Ministry, Government of India, and the lists furnished by the State Governments form the basis. The options of the representatives of various communities, leaders of public opinion and social workers were also taken into consideration.

We thus prepared the lists of other backward classes and also revised the lists of scheduled castes and scheduled tribes. We made every effort to bring in as many communities as possible who answer the criteria but we are conscious that in the conditions prevailing in the country it has not been possible for us to get in touch with some communities who are not well known. Our desire is that such omissions should not come in the way of any community being included later and we suggest that in these cases backwardness be presumed. We have suggested the setting up of a board for the implementation of the policy for the advancement of all the backward classes. This Board should be empowered to investigate the conditions of the communities who may later seek inclusion in the list of other backward classes.

The names of castes have not been specified as Hindu or Muslim and they should invariably be treated as caste names common to both.

CONDITIONS OF BACKWARDNESS AND MEASURES FOR THEIR REMOVAL

Political

The framers of Indian Constitution recognised the historical processes that were at work in India and the uneven development of the various sections of the Indian population. They have, therefore, made adequate provision for the protection and betterment of other backward classes also. Universal adult franchise has given to the masses the most potent and powerful instrument with which to shape their destiny. What is wanted now is the strengthening of their hands through education and not to offer another weapon to weak hands.

After considering all aspects of the question, we have come to the conclusion that it would be suicidal to accord any additional or special political representation to any community or communities.

There are disruptive forces that are trying to entrench themselves by exploiting the prevailing social atmosphere. We suggest that the political parties in the country should take note of the unhealthy symptoms in the body-politic and draw people together under a well-defined economic and social programme.

Economic and Industrial

The objectives should be full employment and the removal of economic inequalities. Maximum production, full employment, the attainment of economic equality and social justice should constitute the accepted objective of planning under the present-day conditions.

Unplanned industrial development in India, urbanisation and expansion of trade and commerce, growth of towns and large cities and the British educational and industrial policy have disrupted the old village economy and have resulted in denuding the rural areas of local talent and leadership.

During the 30 years following 1921 the population has increased by 11 crores, and there is a drop of 25 per cent in the per capita area of cultivated land.

The pressure on land has increased from decade to decade. The decay of rural industries has aggravated the rural situation. All these factors have contributed to the growth of landless agriculturist families.

Smallness of holdings, primitive system of cultivation, lack of educational facilities, lack of adequate agricultural equipment, decay of rural industries causing unemployment and underemployment have all contributed to the present poverty of the rural people.

Any plan for economic reconstruction of the country must necessarily include measures designed for the speedy uplift of the backward classes. Conditions must be recreated in which the development of these classes takes a natural growth. Removal of economic and social causes that are operating to their detriment should receive first priority.

No time should be lost in making fuller use of the human resources, available skill and experience of the artisan and occupational classes to produce goods which are needed by the community. Improved equipment or improved tools and training in modern methods of production may follow the above measures.

The main solution, therefore, for the speedy uplift of the backward classes in the rural area is not so much to wait for the creation of new avenues of employment, as to provide favourable conditions in which their lost or decaying occupations could be revived. A large scale employment in traditional occupations will alone relieve the present pressure on land. It will also help in creating suitable social atmosphere for economic uplift. It is only thereafter that we will have a clear picture of rural life which will enable us to reorganise rural life on a sound and rational bases.

'The economic policy and the ideology behind the Five-Year Plan do not inspire sufficient confidence. It is felt that even the policies enunciated in the Five-Year Plan have not been properly implemented.' The administrative setup entrusted with the task of implementing the welfare measures requires a complete reorientation. There was widespread demand from the representatives of the backward classes that a large number of their own men should be taken into services to bring about better social contact with the masses.

All developmental activities should radiate from central villages of compact blocks consisting of 10 to 15 villages. The country should be divided into compact blocks of such dimensions on a planned basis, and modern amenities should be taken to such Panchkoshi units. The disturbing causes of rural life such as factious feelings, presence of anti-social elements and the habit of litigation often leading to breaches of peace should be removed to help development of the rural areas.

Land Policy

For the uplift of the backward classes, it is vital to have a proper land policy. It is necessary that all kinds of intermediary tenures should be abolished to help in the formulation and implementation of a national land policy.

The land legislation must be simple and easily understandable by the rural population. There should be no loopholes in such a legislation that might lead to social conflict. Too many and frequent changes in land legislation create confusion and difficulty and often lead to endless litigation and exploitation.

Large Landowners and Ceilings on Holdings

The general picture in the country is one of numerous small holdings, a large proportion of them being uneconomic, a small number of middle peasants and a sprinkling of substantial owners. If it were the sole object of policy to reduce the holdings of the large owners with a view to providing for the landless or for increasing the farms of those who now have uneconomic fragments, the facts at present available suggest that these aims are not likely to be achieved in any substantial measure. The principle of an upper limit for land-holdings must be considered in relation to the general economic pattern of the country as a whole, rather than in relation to the possible use that could be made of land in excess of any ceiling limit that may be fixed. Fixing a ceiling on land-holding is necessary as a social principle to remove the existing inequality of the cultivators' holdings in the countryside. But it should be followed almost immediately by placing limits on incomes from other fields of national economy. Only then would it be possible to create a psychological satisfaction among those who are required to surrender their property for the common good. The ceiling should be different for different types of land and conditions of rainfall, types of crop grown, pressure of population, etc., should be taken into consideration in determining the ceilings.

Distribution of Land

The available government land should firstly be distributed among the landless and then among the owners of uneconomic holdings. To this end land revenue rules should be suitably amended. Any infringement of this rule should be severely dealt with by State authorities.

The excess land resumed after fixing the ceilings should also be distributed first among the landless.

The distribution of land should be left in the hands of government officers who should be instructed to implement the government policy in this behalf.

Small and Middle Owners

These groups include almost all backward communities. Their holdings are uneconomic and seriously fragmented. The general aim should be to bring about consolidation of holdings.

Fragmentation beyond a certain limit should be prohibited by law.

Regulation of Tenancy Rights

It is necessary to protect the tenants under large holders from arbitrary eviction and from the levy of unreasonable rent. A limit on the amount of land to be resumed by the owners for personal cultivation is necessary in all cases where ceilings on holdings are not fixed. In cases where ceilings are fixed the tenants may be given the option to acquire the excess land by payment of suitable price in easy instalments. The quantum of rent to be fixed and the security of tenancy should be determined in relation to local conditions.

In the case of small and middle owners and in cases where ceilings are fixed the rights of tenants under such owners should be regulated by simple laws and it must always be open to the owners to resume the land without difficulty at the end of the tenancy period, which may be fixed from five to ten years.

Record of Rights

Peasant proprietorship, however small the holding, will, for some years, be the pattern in most rural areas. The rights of all interests in land should be correctly recorded and maintained.

Agricultural Class Structure

The preponderance of owner-cultivators is the most important and characteristic feature of our agricultural class structure. The economic conditions of communities engaged in agriculture are far from satisfactory and a large majority of them have necessarily to live below subsistence level. Their position has become such that they are inevitably the helpless victims of exploitation. They need State help in abundant measure, not only to improve agriculture which is their mainstay but to bring about general improvement in their living conditions. It is equally necessary to remove all forms of exploitation from rural life, and establish cooperatives on a planned basis – both functional and regional – manned by proper type of persons who would work devotedly for the betterment of the rural people.

Rural Credit and Marketing

We endorse the integrated scheme of rural credit with State partnership recommended by the All-India Rural Credit Survey.

Rural Indebtedness

Agricultural communities habitually run into debt and more so when adverse seasonal conditions prevail. It is necessary that provision should be made either through land marketing societies or through proposed State Bank for long-term credit to redeem them from the clutches of unconscionable money-lenders. Relief from usurious rates of interest is also needed. Scaling down of the debts of impecunious cultivators is equally desirable.

Marketing Facilities

'In the absence of staying power a large number of small farmers compete with each other and the markets witness conditions of occasional glut and scarcity.' They are subject to exploitation at the hands of money-lenders or *mandi*-merchants in marketing their produce. It is, therefore, necessary to establish cooperative marketing societies, regulated markets at suitable centres with warehouse and banking facilities.

Price Support

The conditions of agricultural communities are largely governed by the price they get for their surplus produce. Minimum fair prices should be guaranteed to the cultivators both from the point of view of keeping up agricultural production and of the prosperity of the agricultural communities.

Irrigation

The most effective way of increasing crop production in India is to provide through irrigation an additional source of water supply to the cultivated land. Small and medium irrigation works have an important part to play and they have obvious advantages. In view of the urgency of this problem we recommend that greater attention should be paid to the execution of small and medium irrigation works and to provide irrigation from wells and rivers wherever it is not possible to have tanks and anicuts.

Land Tax Policy

There have been complaints that the present system of land taxation has not been equitable and it is particularly oppressive in the case of uneconomic holdings. The present system has not been based on the capacity of the cultivator to pay the tax. The system of land taxation in its relation to the capacity of the cultivato should be thoroughly examined and an equitable system of taxation be evolved.

Rural Savings

With the increase in agricultural prosperity there should be scope for effecting savings in rural areas. The villagers have to be educated to practise thrift and economy. There is, therefore, need for organising rural savings schemes at village level.

Communities Engaged in the Cultivation of Vegetables and Flowers

There are some distinct communities who are mainly engaged in the cultivation of vegetables and flowers. They are known by different names in different parts of the country. The following steps are recommended to ameliorate their conditions:

1. Enough land should be made available for growing vegetables and fruits. Suburban belts around large towns should be developed for raising fruits and vegetables by organising these communities into cooperatives, especially for the supply of improved seeds and marketing their produce.
2. The exorbitant rents in all cases of tenancies should be scaled down as in the case of other tenancies.
3. Instructions should be given to the young men of these communities on improved methods of fruit and vegetable cultivation.
4. Scholarships should be established for the purpose of training qualified students among them in general horticulture.

Communities Engaged in Growing Betel Vine

Cultivation of betel Wine is mainly confined to one caste which is found all over the country. It is cultivated on small plots of land and the community is generally poor. The greatest difficulty is in the matter of marketing betel leaves. Pan-growers have lost these export markets in Pakistan, Ceylon, Burma and Nepal. The following measures are recommended for their amelioration:

1. Grant of sufficient and suitable land for raising betel vine to members of this community and reduction of oppressive rents.
2. Establishment of cooperatives to grant medium-term loans for the purchase of agricultural implements and manure and for marketing the betel leaves.
3. Exploration of foreign markets by State for betel leaves.
4. Research work for eradication of pests and diseases and for improving the quality of the vines, and the nutritional and medicinal value of Pan.

Realisation of Village Economy

The First Five Year Plan advocates cooperative farming for the rapid reorganisation of village economy. The Planning Commission has also suggested co-operative village management as the ultimate objective.

But the socio-economic structure of the present village life is not congenial for the proper functioning of cooperatives in rural areas. The basic causes hindering the development of the cooperative Spirit must be removed before agriculture could be reorganised on cooperative principles.

A few essential steps are necessary to facilitate such a reorganisation. They are:

1. Prohibition of investment on land as a source of income by persons who are not themselves cultivators or by those who do not reside either in the village in which the land is situated or on the farm.
2. Acquisition of land in a village from persons who own the land but who are themselves not agriculturists and do not reside in the village.
3. Restraint on alienation of land in favour of a non-agriculturist.
4. Reservation of the required extent of land for grazing purpose and for village plantations.
5. Immediate redistribution of the remaining land among the landless agriculturists in the village in the first instance and among the owners of uneconomic holdings next.
6. Consolidation of holdings.
7. Bringing into vogue mutual aid among agriculturists in farm operations.
8. Organisation of multi-purpose cooperative societies for better farming or for distribution of seeds, fertilisers, agricultural equipment for marketing and financing, etc.

Bhoodan Movement

Bhoodan is in essence the application of the principle of non-violence for the acquisition and distribution of land among the landless in the country. This movment has set in motion a great agrarian revolution, and is creating a necessary psychological climate in the country for the establishment of social ownership of land through voluntary and non-violent means. It is trying to influence the psychology of the 'haves' as regards money, power and prestige and to inculcate in them a feeling of social solidarity by asking them to recognise their duty towards the backward people as members of a vast family. Acharya

Vinoba Bhave is teaching the 'haves' to accept the 'have-nots' on a par with one's blood brothers. He is, therefore, not only removing the backwardness of the 'have-nots' but he is also removing the bitterness which the 'have-nots' in their desperation are nursing. This great agrarian revolution is more spiritual in its content. The scope of Bhoodan Movement is widened to include in its scope '*Sampattidan*', '*Shramadan*' and '*Jeevandan*' so necessary for the establishment of a Sarvodaya society. We recommend both to the government and to the nation that they should take up the work of Bhoodan Movement and spread it to all nooks and corners of the country.

Development of Livestock

The development of agriculture is bound up with the development of livestock, for bullocks are the principal motive power used almost universally for agricultural operations. It is important, therefore, that the cattle wealth of the country should be improved. All communities engaged in agriculture are also engaged in rearing livestock. The prosperity of these communities depends on the development of livestock.

The following steps are essential:

1. Segregation of all useless and decrepit cattle and establishment of Gosadans for their upkeep.
2. Large-scale arrangements for the castration of the useless and scrub bulls, to prevent deterioration in the quality of cattle.
3. Cattle-breeding stations to improve the breed of cattle as also to improve the milk-yielding qualities of the cow should be established. All help and encouragement should be given to local breeders to improve their stock.
4. Steps should be taken to conserve the existing pasture land in the interest village cattle.
5. More veterinary institutions should be established.

Dairying

Small-scale dairying is a general feature in rural areas and brings subsidiary income to the agriculturists. Efforts should be made to organise these small producers into cooperative milk unions and to give them monetary help and other assistance needed for developing dairying.

Cattle Insurance

Cattle in India are subject to periodical epidemics and loss of cattle during such epidemics renders agriculturists helpless. They have no other source to depend upon for their livelihood when they lose their cattle. It is necessary to safeguard their interest by sponsoring schemes of cattle insurance.

Sheep and Wool

One community (class of shepherds) is engaged mainly in sheep-breeding. There is great scope for the improvement of sheep – both of wool and mutton type. The present conditions of sheep-breeders are far from satisfactory. Besides establishing regional centres for improving the quality of wool by selective breeding and cross-breeding, it is necessary to make available sufficient breeding areas to the sheep-breeders in several States. Steps should be taken to protect the flocks of sheep from disease and epidemics.

Poultry and Bee-keeping

Poultry and bee-keeping could form an important subsidiary industry for the poorer classes in the rural areas. It would be a source of additional income to them. Improved breeds such as white leg-horn, Rhode-Island, etc., should be introduced in the rural areas. The rural population should also be instructed in the art of bee-keeping and State help extended to popularise it.

Piggery

Communities engaged in pig-rearing are considered as low castes. Some of them have no fixed placed of residence and they move from place to place with their pigs. The State Governments should give more facilities to communities engaged in this occupation and they must be helped to lead a more settled life.

Fisheries

A number of communities are engaged both in inland fishing and in sea-fishing. Some of them are regarded as untouchables. In addition to fishing, some of them are also engaged in plying boats and ferries in inland streams or cargo boats along the coastal areas. Their living conditions are extremely unsatisfactory and they lead a very hard and stenuous life.

Fisheries have to be developed to supply adequate food to the nation. Fishermen should be organised and helped to form multi-purpose cooperative societies. Through these societies they should be helped to build strong boats or buy boats and nets. They should also be enabled to purchase steam-launchers so that they can convey their catch to coastal towns. Facilities for quick and cheap transport including facilities for the preservation of fish should be afforded to them.

The Khalas community could be encouraged to join the Indian Navy.

Agricultural Labour

According to Dr Radha Kumud Mukherjee, the system of land tenure introduced by the British in India was responsible for the growth of agricultural labour population in India. The decay of cottage and rural industries has also contributed its share. The recent Agricultural Labour Enquiry has revealed that 30.4 per cent of the population in rural areas is of agricultural labour. The same inquiry has disclosed that as many as 89 per cent of them are casual workers and the period of unemployment ranges from three to six months.

Agricultural labour forms the most vulnerable section of the population, and the question of rehabilitation of communities in this group should receive the earnest consideration of the government – Central and State. Revival of cottage and rural industries and reorganisation of agriculture would afford greater opportunities for employment of these communities. The redistribution of land among the landless would further improve the economic conditions of these classes.

Minimum Wages

In the case of agricultural labour, we feel that barring a few exceptional cases the fixation of the mimimum wage is desirable. All the facilities granted to industrial labour should also be extended to the agricultural labour. We may not press at present stage for all these amenities. But we do hope that the requirements regarding (1) Minimum wages; (2) Minimum housing; (3) Drinking water supply; (4) Education; and (5) Health facilities will be treated as overdue to these backward classes.

Development of Industries

The Commission is anxious that the conflict between heavy industries on the one hand and cottage and rural industries on the other be removed. It is necessary in establishing industries to avoid the ugly features of the industrial life of the West. It is equally necessary to avoid heavy concentrations of population around urban areas. Steps should be taken to disperse industries all over the country according to a definite plan.

At present communities belonging to backward classes are employed only as unskilled labour in these industries. Training facilities should be provided for these communities to improve their skill. The principle of recruiting and training suitable men from backward communities to higher ranks of service at least in government-controlled industries should be conceded. Introduction of short-term training courses in all industrial establishments is equally necessary.

RURAL AND COTTAGE INDUSTRIES

The conditions of communities engaged in village and cottage industries and other handicrafts are far from satisfactory. During times of unemployment they have to depend either on dole from government or to resort to begging.

There is conflict of opinion between the policy-makers and those entrusted with the implementation of policies. Some of the government servants in the Industries departments in several States do not appear to have much faith in the survival capacity of cottage and rural industries. There interest is at best lukewarm. The present supervisory, administrative and technical staff employed in Industries departments are not drawn from communities connected with traditional rural industries or occupations.

The policy of giving subsidies to sustain these industries is at best only a palliative. The only feasible course would be to remove all factors hindering natural development of these industries and recreate favourable conditions in which these industries could flourish spontaneously. These communities will, by their own exertions try to improve themselves and their conditions if the atmosphere is favourable. With government assistance and help, it will become easier for them not only to improve the technique of production but to organise themselves on modern lines.

KHADI INDUSTRY

Hand-spinning and hand-weaving have been India's traditional village industry.

'The story of the deterioration became total extermination of so universal an industry in Indian villages is written in blood and tears.' Gandhiji made it the Central programme of his constructive activity, and with the rising tide of nationalism, Khadi gained in importance.

The employment potential of this industry is great. It gives part-time and full-employment to lakhs of villagers and in particular, to the poorer sections of backwad classes. There is great scope for the development of khadi industry, particularly in cotton-growing areas of the country, especially where there are no mills. Improved charkhas and improved looms should be introduced to cut down cost and to step up production.

HANDLOOM INDUSTRY

The growth of Indian mill industry has inevitably affected the fortunes of handloom weavers. As the largest cottage industry in India, it occupies a place of prominence in the general economy of the country. Production of handloom cloth has recently been about 1,200 million yards out of a total production in the country of about 6,200 million yards per annum. In spite of great vicissitudes in the economic upheavals this industry has shown great vitality to survive and continues to sustain millions of people. It is estimated that about 100 lakhs of people including dependents are supported by this industry. The tradition, experience, and skill of handloom weavers have been long and distinguished. This could be preserved only by preventing unfair competition by the mills. The well-being of the communities engaged in handloom weaving depends upon the early rehabilitation of this industry. The following measures are recommended for the resuscitation of this industry:

1. Clear demarcation of spheres of production exclusively for the handloom should be made with immediate effect. Since the weavers are accustomed to produce varieties of fabrics like *Saris, Dhotis and Lungis* — all these varieties should be exclusively reserved for the handloom industry. The present partial reservation has not helped the industry to any desirable extent.
2. Regular and adequate supply of yarn of required counts and colours at reasonable prices should be ensured to the handloom weavers. (See in this connection Chairman's note on Ambar yarn).
3. All weavers should be brought into the co-operative fold as soon as possible with a view to protecting them from exploitation by middlemen and master weavers.
4. A chain of marketing organisations should be formed throughout the country and possibilities should be thoroughly explored for creation of foreign markets for handloom fabrics.
5. After full protection and patronage to khadi, only handloom products should be purchased by governments – Central and State – for their requirements.
6. Financial asistance by State should be provided to weavers for the improvement of their looms for increased production.
7. Weavers are at present living and working in 'shocking conditions of congestion.' A planned programme for improving their housing condition and, where necessary, for development of weavers' Colonies is urgently called for and should be undertaken by government without any delay.
8. With improvement in the technique of production of the handloom industry and increase in its yardage, the textile mills should be required gradually to confine themselves to the production of fabrics of exporting varieties as well as of luxury fabrics of finest yarn both for export and for internal consumption.

SPECIAL FEATURES OF COTTON AND SILK WEAVING IN ASSAM AND MANIPUR

Assam and Manipur have strong domestic weaving tradition. In these two States handloom weaving is non-commercial in nature. Women of these two States are expert weavers. Weaving industry here is severely handicapped for want of regular supply of yarn from the mills. There is a great possibility of making Assam and Manipur completely self-sufficient in cloth. To this end, the entry of mill-cloth should be prohibited and the State governments should give special help to hand-spinning and weaving and also set up a yarn mill with required spindleage. Cotton cultivation in some parts of Assam should also be encouraged. These steps should provide a large volume of employment to the backward communities including a large number of tribals.

SILK HANDLOOM INDUSTRY

Silk handloom weavers suffer from the hard competition from the mills. Sudden and sharp fluctuations in the price of silk yarn often throws a good number of them out of employment. Arrangements should be made for supplying those weavers with silk yarn at reasonable prices. The All-India Handloom Board should draw programmes for improving the conditions of weavers and in marketing their cloth.

SERICULTURE

Sericulture is one of the successful cottage industries giving subsidiary employment to a large population of agricultural communities. The internal production of silk is not yet sufficient to meet the country's demand, and the unregulated imports of raw silk from abroad creates crises in the local industry. There is great scope both for expansion and for improvement in the method of production of silk. This industry needs stabilisation and it is only then it can develop sufficiently rapidly.

WOOL SPINNING AND WEAVING INDUSTRY

The wool spinning and weaving industry is mainly confined to a community of shepherds who are found all over the country. Severe mill competition has been responsible for the decay of this industry. Though India is a large producer of wool, a great part of it is exported and the local weaving industry is severely handicapped. Proper organisations should be set up preferably on cooperative lines in suitable places for the purchase and supply of wool to the spinners and weavers. Marketing facilities for the sale of woollen blankets should be provided so that weavers may get proper price for their products. It is also necessary to improve the technique of softening wool and of production of both woollen yarn and blankets to suit the changing tastes of the people. Woollen cloths should be standardised to supply the needs of the Defence Forces and Hospitals.

VILLAGE OIL INDUSTRY

The village oil industry is mostly in the hands of the community of *Telis*. The number of workers engaged in this industry has been falling steadily from decade to decade. The oil mill industry has affected this industry to a geat extent and a large number of *telis* are either unemployed or have joined the ranks of agricultural labour.

India is one of the most important producers of oil seeds and yet the tragedy of the situation is that the traditional oil pressers find it difficult to sustain their industry in the face of competition from oil mill industry. Both from the point of view of employment and of improving the conditions of village *telis*, it is essential to reserve the crushing of edible oil seeds to the village *ghanis*. Initially if the competition is removed and the regular supply of oil seeds ensured, the *telis* themselves will immediately revive the industry. This may follow supply of improved *ghanis* and the organisation for the supply of oil seeds and for marketing oil produced by the village oil industry. We would add that immediate steps should be taken to stop the use of machinery for crushing edible oil. It is also necessary to stop further licensing of new oil mills and gradually stop the crushing of edible oils in the existing mills.

VILLAGE POTTER

The community of village potters have preserved the traditional art of producing not only artistic and elegant earthenware but also articles for the daily use of all the poor and backward communities. At present they find no place in the production of modern ceramic wares. The potters should be encouraged to improve their methods of production by giving them training and better implements.

BAMBOO AND CANE WORKERS

Communities engaged in bamboo and cane works are known by different names in different States. They are poor and backward, and live in segregated areas in villages or in the vicinity of forests. Their main difficulties are lack of raw materials at reasonable prices and proper marketing facilities. In view of the wide variety of bamboo and cane in our country there is unlimited scope for the improvement in the production of articles from bamboo and cane to suit modern tastes. Steps should be taken to encourage these communities by arranging supply of raw materials at reasonable prices and proper marketing facilities. Proper housing and educational facilities should be provided for improving the conditions of the people.

PADDY HUSKING

The establishment of rice mills has greatly affected this important village industry. Paddy husking is a source of employment to a large number of agricultural labourers and it is stated that 65% of paddy is still hand-pounded and hasked locally. It is desirable to eliminate rice mills altogether from the rural areas.

COIR INDUSTRY

Coir industry is still providing a large volume of employment in Travancore-Cochin, but is often subject to periodical depression. The recent setting up of Coir Board is expected to help this industry.

MINOR INDUSTRIES

Communities engaged in preparing leaf-plates, collecting lac from forests, etc. are poor and backward. Special measures should be taken for their uplift and rehabilitation.

VILLAGE HANDICRAFTS

There is always a large and popular demand for articles of utility produced by village artisans. Factory's products have affected the production if village artisans. The latter need protection and assistance at the hands of the public and the States. Care must be taken to distinguish between artisans who produce useful articles and those who produce works of fine arts. Those works of art cannot be produced on a mass scale. With disappearance of Kings, Maharajas, Nawabs and Zamindars, the traditional patronage is gone. These artisan classes should be assisted and encouraged and National Museums of Art and Emporia should be established to patronise these artists. The governments should purchase these articles of art to adorn the Embassies, Parliament and Legislatures. The Government of India should assist in building up foreign markets for such articles.

BEEDI INDUSTRY

The Beedi industry has a great potentiality for the employment of labour. Steps are necessary not only to prevent exploitation but also to organise beedi workers on a co-operative basis.

MILL AND FACTORY COMPETITION

Protection of cottage and rural industries from unrestricted competition of the mills and factories and decentralisation of industries will greatly contribute towards rehabilitation of backward classes.

COMMUNITIES WHOSE TRADITIONAL OCCUPATION IS PERSONAL SERVICE

They are the washerman, the barber, the Kahar or the water-carrier and other classes of domestic servants. The conditions of these communities are far from satisfactory. They need special help for ameliorating their conditions.

WANDERING COMMUNITIES

There are a number of small communities who eke out a precarious existence in the countryside. They have no fixed place of residence and they move from place to place in search of food and employment. They believe in witch-craft. Because of the insecurity of their lives, some of these communities are driven to crime. It should be the special responsibility of the government to give them a settled life.

TRADITIONAL BEGGARS

Ancient tradition has dignified a life of mendicancy. It enjoined that only those who accepted selfless service as a life mission were entitled to live on alms. This ideal was too good to remain unsullied. People who did not want to work for their bread assumed the name of religion and took to begging. Famines and invasions sometimes eracted a large band of beggars. Hinduism enjoined feeding the poor as one of the duties of the house-holder. India, therefore, contentedly maintained a large body of beggars till at last the institution broke under its own weight. The caste system also must share the responsibility for a large number of beggars. Some communities claim that beggary is their traditional profession and that they cannot take to any service, occupation or industry. Society has to consider the whole situation and tackle the problem by insisting on certain social standards being accepted universally both by those who accept alms and those who give them. What is needed most is that the ideal of self-respect and the concept of dignity of labour should be instilled into the minds of the people. It is only by direct inculcation of social ideals that beggary can be effaced and the man-power of India fully utilised.

MEASURES TO PREVENT EXPLOITATION OF THE BACKWARD CLASSES

Backward classes are subject to various kinds of exploitation. Measures to save them from exploitation are absolutely essential for the improvement of their economic conditions.

Proper institutions must be set up for the distribution of wealth produced. A chain of suitable co-operative institutions or government stores is badly needed for this purpose. Steps should be taken to train these communities in running institutions set up for their benefit.

The ultimate solution seems to be that all production and distribution should be on a socialistic basis and that people should be encouraged to establish the necessary moral basis and to get trained for the change over.

COMMUNICATIONS

India is a land of vast distances and unless all kinds of communications are developed it will not be possible to remove either the backwardness of areas cut off from urban centres or of people inhabiting these areas.

PUBLIC HEALTH AND RURAL WATER SUPPLY

Backward class communities generally live in insanitary conditions and in ill-ventilated houses. Ideas of sanitation and public health among them are still primitive. Large scale preventive measures are necessary to improve the health of these classes. It is absolutely essential that the rural public should be educated in the necessity of maintaining sanitary conditions.

Rural water-supply should be improved a great deal. Public wells and reservoirs must be built within the easy reach of the Harijan quarters for the use of the whole area. These should be maintained in sanitary conditions under the supervision of a Village Water Committee with a Harijan as President.

RURAL HOUSING

The housing conditions of many of the communities belonging to backward classes are far from satisfactory. They live in ill-ventilated mud houses of thatched sheds. These houses are generally overcrowded.

A planned programme of rural housing should be drawn up to provide housing for the poorer sections in proper village layouts. Sites for building houses should be made available to those people either free or at nominal rates. Financial assistance either in the form of subsidies or loans should also be given to help the backward communities to construct cheap houses. Housing co-operatives may be organised for this purpose.

SOCIAL BACKWARDNESS AND MEASURES FOR ITS REMOVAL

Social backwardness of many communities of the backward class group is due to the undesirable features of the Hindu social system. The sense of caste and discrimination based on social inequality is eating into the vitals of the nation. Modern conditions no doubt, are gradually toning down some of those rigid caste ideas but the spirit of caste still permeates the major ranks of our society. In condemning the inequitous features of the caste system, it is not suggested that Hinduism should be liquidated. Hinduism could be purified or cleansed of the dross which it has accumulated during the course of centuries. Hinduism must re-examine itself in the world context and boldly shed all its undesirable features. It must cease to be mediaeval in its concept of life; must refresh itself and take a new form which would liberate the spirit of man and enable him to assimilate the best and the noblest that Hinduism has treasured through the ages.

The Hindu view of life was based on a harmonious pursuit of the four chief conceivable objects, viz. *Dharma, Artha, Kama and Moksha.* It taught the universal brotherhood of man, or rather the essential unity of mankind as all individual beings were regarded as part of one Eternal Soul.

The process of equalisation is beset with many hazards. Poverty, ignorance and illiteracy make the task all the more difficult. Therefore, nothing short of a firm determination by the entire nation and in particular by the leaders of society to effect a complete revolution in the fundamental social outlook of the people can possibly fuse the diverse elements into a homogeneous society.

We indicate below, on general lines, the measures that the governments — Central and State — should undertake for the eradication of social evils:

1. A clear enunciation and effective implementation of this policy of social solidarity and national progress.
2. Necessary legislation on marriage and inheritance laws.
3. Prohibition by law of social disabilities.
4. Arrangements for the production and distribution of literature on social problems.
5. Liberal use of the Press, Films, Platform and Radio for the removal of social evils.
6. Prohibition of all observances tending to promote caste feelings in governmental activities.
7. Re-organisation of the educational system with special emphasis on the dignity of manual labour.
8. Full assistance to promote education as speedily as possible among the backward classes.
9. Adequate representation in government service and government controlled industrial establishments of those sections who had no chance so far.
10. Encouragement to art, literature, special cultural groups and assistance and promotion of cultural activities with this social end in view.

EDUCATIONAL BACKWARDNESS AND MEASURES FOR ITS REMOVAL

The following are the various causes of educational backwardness of the backward classes:

1. Traditional apathy for education on account of social and environmental conditions or occupational handicaps.
2. Poverty and lack of means of a large number of communities to educate their children.
3. Lack of educational institutions in the rural areas.
4. Living in inaccessible areas and lack of proper communications.
5. Lack of adequate educational aids in the form of free-ships, scholarships and monetary grants for the purchase of books and clothing.
6. Lack of residential hostel facilities in places where educational institutions are situated.
7. Unemployment among the educated acting as a damper on the desire of some of the communities to educate their children.
8. Defective educational system which does not train students for appropriate occupations and social professions.

The general progress of literacy in India is slow and literacy among the backward classes is appallingly low. Introduction of free and compulsory elementary education is imperative to wipe off illiteracy from among the backward classes. In recommending immediate introduction of free and compulsory education for the age group 6-14 we are not advocating the extension of the present orthodox system of education. We are in favour of immediate conversion of the existing elementary schools into basic schools and the establishment of only basic schools wherever there are no schools.

The teachers for the basic schools should be drawn from the artisan and occupational communities in the rural areas. They must be trained in general education and then posted as teachers. The establishment of basic schools should be on a planned basis and central villages should be selected for the location of senior basic schools so that they could serve all the feeder villages within a radius of five miles. Each *Panchkoshi* area should have a small Board or Committee whose responsibility it would be to see that no child in that area went without basic education.

Non-communal hostels should be established and the cost of board and lodging for the poorer sections of the backward classes should be borne by the government. Students of all communities and all religious denominations should be encouraged to live together and to lead a common life. It should be possible for such teachers and students to live together, work together, and study together.

Special type of Ashram schools (*Samata Ashrams*) where teachers with their families live with the students should be established. One such *Ashram* school in each one of the 300 and odd districts into which India is divided should be established. These Ashrams should be run by special trained teachers who have equal respect for all religions and who regard all communities as belonging to one human family.

The *Panchkoshi* schools as also *Samata Ashrams* will naturally culminate into rural universities of the basic type.

In order to make basic education popular with the masses and to carry conviction with them, it is necessary that government should categorically declare that in selecting candidates for government service, especially of the upper grades, students trained in basic education will be given a decided preference.

Pre-basic or pre-school education is necessary to overcome the initial social handicap under which the backward classes children are suffering.

The secondary stage of education is vital from the point of view of the educational advancement of the backward classes. Until suitable senior basic schools are established, there is need to start secondary schools in rural areas. Hostels should be attached to the secondary schools on non-communal lines. But it is necessary that a majority of the places in those hostels should be reserved for the boys belonging to backward classes. The aim should be to make the hostels training grounds for developing that common social outlook which is so necessary for the future well-being of the country.

UNIVERSITY EDUCATION

Since the Basic Rural Universities would gradually take their place, the present-day Universities should confine themselves to technical education and research, certain percentage of seats being reserved for qualified students of the backward classes and liberal scholarships being granted to poorer amongst them.

POST-GRADUATE COURSES AND RESEARCH CENTRES IN INDIA AND ABROAD

Adequate provision should be made both by the State and the Central Governments for training students of all backward classes in post-graduate courses and in research centres both in India and abroad.

ADULT EDUCATION

In the interests of the backward classes, the scheme of social education should be expanded to cover the whole country, priority being given to those areas where the standard of literacy is low.

RURAL READING ROOMS AND LIBRARIES

Reading rooms and libraries in rural areas should be established and a judicious selection of books be made for stocking rural libraries. Import and periodicals should be read out in the rural reading rooms to keep the people in touch with the day-to-day happenings in the country. Also seminal books should be read out before serious adults and explained.

ALL INDIA INSTITUTIONS FOR HIGHER LEARNING

In order to achieve speedy educational advancement of the backward classes and to create new conditions to root out casteism and regional and linguistic tendencies, special residential institutions of the university grade should be set up in various States to inculcate an All India outlook among the students. These institutions should be manned by professors and lecturers of learning and patriotism. The courses of studies should be suitably devised. The medium of instruction should be Hindi but one or two original languages must also be taught. Professors and students drawn from all parts of the country and from all communities should live, study and work together.

Government should spend all money on basic education and only where basic schools cannot be started for want of teachers money may be spent on orthodox education.

FACILITIES FOR ADVANCED STUDIES ABROAD

Government of India should make adequate provision for award of various scholarships to backward class students.

SCHEME OF SCHOLARSHIPS IN STATES

(a) Schemes for freeships and scholarships should be introduced in all the States for the benefit of students belonging to other backward classes. The State Governments should make adequate provision in their budgets for the purpose.

(b) In awarding scholarships the claims of all communities among the backward classes should be taken into consideration and the allotment in the first instance should be on the basis of population of various communities in a State, preference being given always to those who are extremely backward, viz., starred communities, in the lists prepared by the Commission.

(c) Small committees consisting of representatives of various communities be constituted for various grades of scholarships in each State to assist the educational authorities to select deserving candidates from among the various communities for purposes of award.

(d) General income of the parents of a student applying for a scholarship should not exceed Rs. 1,800 per annum to enable him to get a scholarship up to the secondary course.

(e) In all cases of education abroad, income of the parents of a student should not exceed Rs. 3,600 per annum for getting a scholarship.

RESERVATION OF SEATS IN SCIENCE, MEDICINE, ENGINEERING, AGRICULTURE, VETERINARY AND OTHER TECHNICAL AND TECHNOLOGICAL INSTITUTIONS OF HIGHER LEARNING

(a) In all Science, Engineering, Medicine, Agriculture, Veterinary and other technical and technological institutions, a reservation of 70 per cent of seats should be made for qualified students of backward classes till such time as accommodation is provided for all the students eligible for admission. The remaining 30 per cent as also all seats unavailed of by backward classes should go to the rest of the students.

(b) In making selecting to the reserved quota of seats, qualified candidates from extremely backward classes should be taken into consideration first, and in making distribution, the principle of favouring the lower of the two claimants among the candidates from the various communities should be followed.

(c) A Selection Committee consisting of some of the representatives of all Communities (not necessarily, of the backward alone) should be set up to assist the educational authorities in the selection of deserving candidates.

REPRESENTATION OF O.B.Cs. IN GOVERNMENT SERVICE — CENTRAL AND STATES

(i) Prestige, power and influence, scales of pay, security of employment and scope to distribute patronage — all these have made government service attractive. So long as it continues to be so, claims of O.B.Cs. for adequate representation in the service should be recognised by providing reservation of definite quota of vacancies in each class.

(ii) To lessen the keen desire for government services on the part of the O.B.Cs. one way is to render them as unattractive as possible by reducing the emoluments attached to them. Social justice and communal harmony both demand that the present alarming disparity between the scales of pay of the lowest and the highest appointments should be reduced. As an immediate step, the ratio between the emoluments of the lowest and those of the highest paid pesons may be reduced to 1 : 20. But this ratio may be ultimately brought down to 1 : 10.

(iii) Keeping in view the necessity for maintaining high administrative efficiency in conjunction with social justice to all sections of the population, best candidates should, as a rule, be recruited by means of a competitive examination without any regard to caste considerations.

(iv) Even in the sector of reservation, the best amongst the qualified backward classes should be recruited. The method of recruitment to this sector could be either by personal interview and nomination or by open competition. In the latter case the selection should be confined to the best among those satisfying the required standard in the examination despite their lower ranks in the general list.

(v) Whatever the procedure of recruitment, whether through selection after personal interview or by limited competition amongst the candidates of backward communities, the reservation specified must be secured in favour of candidates of the O.B.C. group. Strict adherence to rules of recruitment, with a severe penalty for any breach thereof, would be the best remedy.

(vi) The interest of the State, the efficiency and the running of the administrative machinery and the increasing role of welfare which the administrative services have to play in relation to masses of the country — all these demand that reservation should, where education is sufficiently high among the communities, be in proportion to the population of the communities of the other backward classes. Taking all these factors into consideration the conclusion reached by a majority of the members of the Commission is that in all government and Local Body Services, the minimum basis of representation of O.B.Cs. should be as follows:

Class I 25 per cent of vacancies.
Class II 33-1/3 per cent of vacancies.
Class III 40 per cent of vacancies.
Class IV 40 per cent of vacancies.

This percentage would be over and above that which has already been conceded by government in the case of scheduled castes and scheduled tribes.

(vii) At the end of 10 years the adequacy of representation of O.B.Cs. should be reviewed in the light of the statistics then available as a result of the 1961 or earlier census which may contain all communities listed by the Commission in the O.B.Cs. group.

(viii) For purposes of distribution of the reserved quota of posts among all the communities comprising the O.B.Cs. no hard and fast rule need be followed. The circumstances and the social conditions prevailing in the country necessitate greater consideration for the most backward and unrepresented communities in the group. Some system of rotation worked out in the conditions prevailing in the respective State is called for. Communities should be conveniently grouped according to the degree of advancement in each State and representation in the reserved quota be granted beginning with the most unrepresented groups. This method need not be adhered to for all time. After a period of 15 years the position should be reviewed.

(ix) While recognising the desirability of selecting the best qualified candidates in technical services, the O.B.Cs., should be increasingly given facilities in educational and more especially in technical institutions. It should be the definite policy for many years to come that, qualifications being fairly equal, preference should be given to a candidate from among the backward classes.

(x) Where training is needed to improve efficiency among the candidates belonging to backward classes after selection to various posts, they should be given training for a year or two during the period of probation.

(xi) While in the selection of members for Public Service Commission appointments from among the members of backward classes should continue on as liberal a scale as possible. Caste or community consideration should have no place whatsoever in making the selection. Merit should be the sole criterion.

(xii) A Board consisting of a small body of trained and experienced administrators and social workers should be set up with sufficient powers to enforce full and proper implementation of the policy for recruitment to government service and also to consider any complaints from non-backward classes in the unreserved sector of employment under government service. The precise powers and functions of the Board should be carefully worked out by government.

MINISTRY FOR THE ADVANCEMENT OF BACKWARD CLASSES

(i) A new Ministry should be created both at the Centre and in the States similar to the Ministry of Rehabilitation to handle in an effective manner the problems for the advancement of backward classes and also to prevent anti-social elements from fostering disruptive tendencies among the backward classes by exploiting discontentment among them.

(ii) This Ministry should have sufficient powers to co-ordinate ameliorative measures and welfare work done through different agencies in the various States. In particular, the following should be its special functions:-

(a) All educational problems
(b) Rural housing schemes
(c) Representation in services under Govt. and Local Bodies
(d) Administration of grants for welfare measures
(e) Provision of full employment in rural areas
(f) Drawing up schemes for the advancement of backward classes
(g) Provision of adequate finances for implementation

(iii) A department consisting of distinct sections each administering separately the affairs of scheduled castes, scheduled tribes and other backward classes should be placed under the new Ministry. Sanctioning of schemes, allotment of funds, co-ordination of work, training of personnel etc. would be the main functions of the Department. Funds should be separately earmarked for each of the three categories of the backward classes, namely scheduled castes, scheduled tribes and other backward classes and the expenditure should also be separately debited.

(iv) Constitution of an Advisory Board

(a) An advisory Board both at the Centre and in each State to assist the new Ministry in the administration of welfare measures should also be set up.
(b) Major question of policy and specific schemes for uplift should be placed before this Board for eliciting opinion.
(c) The powers and functions of the Board should be worked out in detail by the Government of India.

GRANTS

A statement containing a summary of the recommendations in respect of financial grants required to give effect to various ameliorative measures will be found at the end of Chapter VIII of the Report.

REVISION OF LISTS OF SCHEDULED CASTES AND SCHEDULED TRIBES

(i) General — Members of scheduled castes and scheduled tribes when they go from one State to another should receive the amount of their help that is given to other backward classes in the State where they have gone to reside.

(ii) The whole State should be one unit for purposes of help to scheduled tribes and the help offered to tribal people should be given to them irrespective of their shifting from one area to another in the State.

(iii) Scheduled Tribes.

Assam — An exhaustive investigation of the tribes and their conditions in Assam should be made. Various agencies like Tribal Research Institution under the Government of India or under Universities may profitably be made use of for this purpose. Government may co-ordinate the work done by these agencies to collect more reliable data of various tribes of Assam. All the tribes should be listed by their own particular names in the hilly areas of Assam and Manipur.

Uttar Pradesh — Tribes found in Uttar Pradesh should be included in the list of scheduled tribes.

Himachal Pradesh — Gaddis and Gujars in Himachal Pradesh who lead a tribal life should be given help not only to improve the breed of their cattle but also amenities and rest houses both for men and cattle on the way when they go to plains during winter months.

Rajasthan — Nomadic tribes who are breeders of cattle in Rajasthan should be given necessary assistance.

public; extensive touring of the country by the Commission, taking evidence of legislators, eminent publicmen, sociologists, etc.; undertaking a country-wide socio-educational survey; preparation of reports on some important issues by specialised agencies; analysis of census data, etc.

By adopting this multilateral approach the Commission was able to cast its net far and wide and prepared a very firm and dependable data, base for its Report.

Chapter IV — Social Backwardness and Caste

Castes are the building bricks of the Hindu social structure. They have kept Hindu society divided in a hierarchical order for centuries. This has resulted in a close linkage between the caste ranking of a person and his social, educational and economic status.

This manner of stratification of society gave the higher castes deep-rooted vested interests in the perpetuation of the system. The priestly castes evolved an elaborate and subtle scheme of scripture, ritual and mythology and perpetuate their supremacy and hold the lower castes in bondage for ages. Most of our Shastras uphold the four-fold Varna system and, because of this religious sanction, caste system has lasted longer than most other social institutions based on inequality and inequity.

In view of the permanent stratification of society in hierarchical caste order, members of lower castes have always suffered from discrimination in all walks of life and this has resulted in their social, educational and economic backwardness. In India, therefore, the low ritual caste status of a person has a direct bearing on his social backwardness.

Chapter V — Social Dynamics of Caste

Caste system has been able to survive over the centuries because of its inherent resilience and its ability to adjust itself to the even changing social reality. The traditional view of caste system, as contained in Chapter IV, is based more on Hindu Shastras than the actual state of social reality. Moreover, caste restrictions have loosened considerably as a result of the rule of law introduced by the British, urbanisation, industrialisation, spread of mass education and, above all, the introduction of adult franchise after Independence. But all the above changes mark only shift of emphasis and not any material alternation in the basic structure of caste.

It is generally agreed that whereas certain caste taboos have weakened as a result of the above changes, the importance of casteism in Indian politics is on the increase. This perhaps, was inevitable. Caste system provided the political leadership with readymade channels of communication and mobilisation and, in view of this, the importance of caste was bound to increase in Indian politics. As Rajni Kothari has observed, 'those in India who complain of 'casteism' in politics are really looking for a sort of politics which has no basis in society.'

The pace of social mobility is no doubt increasing and some traditional features of caste system have inevitably weakened. But what caste has lost on the ritual front, it has more than gained on the political front. In view of this it will be unrealistic to assume that the institution of caste will wither away in the foreseeable future.

Chapter VI — Social Justice, Merit and Privilege

Equality before the law is a basic Fundamental Right guaranteed under Article 14 of the Constitution. But the principle of 'equality' is a double-edged weapon. It places the strong and the handicapped on the same footing in the race of life. It is a dictum of social justice that there is equality only among equals. To treat unequals as equals is to perpetuate inequality. The humaneness of a society is determined by the degree of protection it provides to its weaker, handicapped and less gifted members.

'Equality of opportunity' and 'equality of treatment' places the weak and the strong on par and, to that extent, it amounts to denial of social justice. In fact, it is 'equality of results' which is the acid test of society's egalitarian pretentions. In a highly unequal society like ours, it is only by giving special protection and privileges to the under-privileged section of society that we can enable the weak to resist exploitation by the strong.

It was in view of these considerations that our Constitution makers made special provisions under Articles 15(4), 16(4) and 46 etc. to protect the interests of SCs, STs and OBCs. Some people consider provisions like reservation of posts for backward classes, etc., as a violation of their Fundamental Right and denial of meritorious person's legitimate due. In fact, 'merit' itself is largely a product of favourable environmental privileges and higher rating in an examination does not necessarily reflect higher intrinsic worth of the examinee. Children of socially and educationally backward parents coming from rural background cannot compete on an equal footing with children from well to do homes. In view of this 'merit' and 'equality' should be viewed in proper perspective and the element of privilege should be duly recognised and discounted for when 'unequals' are made to run the same race.

Chapter VII — Social Justice, Constitution and the Law

The element of conflict between the Fundamental Rights and the Directive Principles of State Policy has been the subject-matter of numerous Parliamentary debates and judicial pronouncements. In pursuance of Articles 15(4) and 16(4) a number of State Governments made reservations in government services and educational institutions for OBCs and several petitions were filed before the High Courts and the Supreme Court against such orders. Gradually a sizeable body of case law has grown on the subject and a gist of it is given below.

Caste is an important factor in the identification of other backward classes among Hindu communities. Backwardness must be both social and educational and not either social or educational. Caste is also a class of citizens and if the caste as a whole is socially and educationally backward, reservation can be made in favour of such a caste on the ground that it is a socially and educationally backward class of citizens within the meaning of Article 15(4). The further division of backward classes into 'backward' and 'most backward' is not warranted by Article 15(4). The aggregate reservation of posts under article 15(4) should be less than 50 per cent. Objective criteria should be evolved on the basis of field survey, etc. for identifying OBCs.

Chapter VIII — North South Comparison of OBC Welfare

Southern States have done much more for the welfare of other backward classes (OBCs) than Northern States. Moreover, in the South the whole operation was conducted quite smoothly whereas in the North even modest welfare measures for OBCs have given rise to sharp resistance. The Commission approached Tata Institute of Social Sciences, Bombay, to prepare a comparative study of the 4 States of Tamil Nadu, Karnataka, Bihar and Uttar Pradesh, so as to have better appreciation of this phenomenon.

Tata Institute Study formulated a number of hypotheses in this regard. They are : Reservation scheme had a much longer history in the South; forward castes were more divided among themselves in the South; OBCs were not getting along very well with SCs/STs in the North and thus divided the backward classes movement; backward classes were more politicised in the South; reservation scheme was introduced too suddenly in the North; the capacity of backward classes to retaliate depends upon their numbers, political consciousness, dominance and perceived lack of alternative opportunities; more rapid expansion of tertiary sector gave opening to forward castes in the South which was not available to the same extent in the North, etc.

Tata Institute Study supports the above hypotheses by citing a number of examples and historical developments in the 4 States under consideration.

Chapter IX — Evidence by Central and State Governments

Two sets of questionnaires were circulated to all State Governments, Union Territories and Ministries and Departments of Central Government for eliciting information on various aspects of our inquiry. These questionnaires were designed to obtain a comparative picture of status of backward classes in various States, steps taken for their welfare, views of various government agencies on the question of social and educational backwardness and any useful suggestions regarding the Commission's terms of reference.

Most of the State Governments favoured caste as an important criterion for determining social and educational backwardness. Some States preferred economic criterion and some a combination of caste and means-test. Eighteen State Governments and Union Territories have taken special steps for the welfare of other backward classes, though there is wide variation in the quantum of assistance provided by them. For instance, reservation in government services for OBCs ranges from 50 per cent in the case of Karnataka and Tamil Nadu and 5 per cent in Punjab and nil in the case of Rajasthan, Orissa, Delhi, etc. Representation of OBCs in local bodies, State Public Service

Commission, High Courts, etc., is also negligible. Social discrimination is still practised against OBCs. There are a number of castes and communities which are treated as untouchables though they have not been included in the list of scheduled castes. All the State Governments which have launched programmes for the welfare of backward classes have to fund the same from their own resources as no separate Plan allocation is made by the Centre for this purpose.

Most States have reported loss of employment by village artisans owing to the introduction of machines, change in consumption patterns, etc.

From the information supplied by the Central Government Ministries and Departments it is seen that other backward classes constitute 12.55 per cent of the total number of government employees, whereas their aggregate population is 52 per cent. Their representation in Class I jobs is only 4.69 per cent *i.e.*, less than 1/10th of their proportion to the country's total population.

Chapter X — Evidence by the Public

Nearly 2/3rd of the respondents to our questionnaire for General Public felt that no material changes have taken place in the country's caste structure since Independence. Regarding criterion for identifying backwardness, nearly 3/4th of the respondents favoured caste. More than 3/4th of the respondents also complained of various disabilities suffered by backward classes and many felt that no concrete steps have been taken to remove them. They wanted job reservation quotas to be enhanced ana more educational concessions to be given to the children of OBC. Ameliorative measures suggested for OBCs were : reservation in government employment and educational institutions; grant of interest free loans, free distribution of agricultural land and house sites; etc.

In their evidence before the Commission, Members of Sixth and Seventh Lok Sabha also expressed views similar to those summarised above. Some MPs warned against malicious propaganda being carried on by vested interests to create conflict between OBCs and SCs and STs. Some stated that the Commission should adopt those criteria for determining backwardness which have been tested before the Courts. They also suggested that the lists of OBCs prepared by State Governments and accepted by the Courts should be adopted by the

Commission *in toto*.

During the Commission's tour to various States, a large number of representations were received for including particular castes in the list of OBCs. Most of the other respondents expressed similar views on the criterion for identifying backward classes and measures to be taken for their upliftment as already indicated above.

Chapter XI — Socio-Educational Field Survey — Criteria for Backwardness

A country-wide socio-educational survey covering 405 out of 407 Districts was conducted with the help of Bureau of Economics and Statistics of various States from February to June 1980. Voluminous data gathered from the Survey were computerised and 31 primary tables were generated from these data in respect of each State and Union Territory. On the basis of these tables, 11 Indicators or Criteria for social and educational backwardness were derived and they were grouped under 3 broad heads, *i.e.*, Social, Educational and Economic. In view of their relative importance, 3 points were assigned to each one of the Social Indicators, 2 to Educational Indicators and 1 to Economic Indicators. This added up to a total score of 22 points. All these 11 indicators were applied to each one of the castes covered by the Survey in each State. Castes obtaining a minimum score of 11 points on this scale were listed as socially and educationally backward.

Chapter XII — Identification of OBCs

A large number of castes were identified as backward in each State as a result of the Socio-Educational Survey. As this Survey covered only two villages and one urban block per District, a large number of castes were naturally left out. Moreover, in some cases, the size of the sample was so small that the results were not dependable.

In view of this, two supplementary approaches were adopted to prepare complete lists of OBCs for each State. First, State-wise list of the 11 groups of primitive tribes, exterior castes, criminal tribes, etc. contained in the Registrar General of India's compilation of 1961 were culled and included in the Commission's lists of OBCs. This was done as the social and educational status of these castes and communities was more or less akin to scheduled castes and scheduled tribes.

Secondary, based on the public evidence and personal knowledge of the Members of the Commission, State-wise list of those OBCs were drawn up which could not be covered by the socio-educational survey.

It was a result of this three pronged approach that State lists of OBCs (Volume III) were prepared.

From the results of the field survey it was seen that some of the well-known OBCs which were also included in the lists of backward classes notified by various State Governments were not ranked as 'backward' in the survey. This is unavoidable in any sociological survey based on Statistical methods. Such aberrations were corrected in the light of the other field evidence available with the Commission.

The set of eleven Indicators (criteria), being caste-based, could not be applied to non-Hindu communities. In view of this, a separate set of three criteria was evolved for the identification of non-Hindu backward communities.

On the basis of the available census data, the population of Hindu and non-Hindu OBCs was estimated to be 52 per cent of the total population of India. This is in addition to the population of scheduled castes and scheduled tribes which amounts to 22.5 per cent.

Chapter XIII — Recommendations

Reservation for SCs and STs is in proportion to their population, *i.e.*, 22.5 per cent. But as there is a legal obligation to keep reservations under Articles 15(4) and 16(4) of the Constitution below 50 per cent, the Commission recommends a reservation of 27 per cent for OBCs. This reservation should apply to all government services as well as technical and professional institutions, both in the Centre and the States.

Special educational facilities designed at upgrading the cultural environment of the students should be created in a phased manner in selected areas containing high concentration of OBCs. Special emphasis should be placed on vocational training. Separate coaching facilities should be provided in technical and professional institutions to OBC students to enable them to catch up with students from open quota.

Special programmes for upgrading the skills of village artisans should be prepared and subsidised loans from financial institutions granted to them for setting up small scale industries. To promote the participation of OBCs in the industrial and business life of the country, a separate network of financial and technical institutions should be created by all State Governments.

Under the existing scheme of production-relations, Backward Classes comprising mainly small land-holders, tenants, agricultural labour, village artisans, etc., are heavily dependent on the rich peasantry for their sustenance. In view of this, OBCs continue to remain in mental and material bondage of the dominant castes and classes. Unless these production-relations are radically altered through structural changes and progressive land reforms implemented rigorously all over the country, OBCs will never become truly independent. In view of this, highest priority should be given to radical land reforms by all the States.

At present no Central assistance is available to any State for implementing any welfare measures for other backward classes. Several State Governments expressed their helplessness in undertaking more purposeful development programmes for backward classes in view of lack of resources. It is, therefore, recommended that welfare programmes specially designed for OBCs should be financed by the Central Government in the same manner and to the same extent as done in the case of SCs and STs.

RECOMMENDATIONS

It may appear that the upliftment of other backward classes (OBCs) is part of the larger national problem of the removal of mass poverty. This is only partially correct. The deprivation of OBCs is a very special case of the larger national issue: here the basic question is that of social and educational backwardness and poverty is only a direct consequence of these two crippling caste-based handicaps. As these handicaps are embedded in our social structure, their removal will require far-reaching structural changes. No less important will be changes in the perception of the problems of OBCs by the ruling classes of the country.

Reservations

One such change in the attitude of the ruling elite pertains to the provision of reservation in government services and educational institutions for the candidates of other backward classes. It is generally argued that looking to the large population of OBCs (52%), recruitment of a few thousand OBCs every year against reserved vacancies is not going to produce any perceptible impact on their general condition. On the other hand, the induction of a large proportion of employees against reserved vacancies will considerably impair the quality and efficiency of the government services. It is also stated that the benefits of such reservations will be skimmed off by those sections of OBCs which are already well off and the really backward sections will be left high and dry. Another argument advanced against this approach is that the policy of large scale reservations will cause great heart burning to those meritorious candidates whose entry into services will be barred as a result thereof.

All the above arguments are based on fairly sound reasoning. But these are also the arguments advanced by the ruling elite which is keen on preserving its privileges. Therefore, like all such reasoning, it is based on partisan approach. By the same token, while illuminating some immediate areas of concern it tends to ignore much larger issues of national importance.

It is not all our contention that by offering a few thousand jobs to OBC candidates we shall be able to make 52 per cent of the Indian population as forward. But we must recognise that an essential part of the battle against social backwardness is to be fought in the minds of the backward people. In India government service has always been looked upon as a symbol of prestige and power. By increasing the representation of OBCs in government services, we given them an immediate feeling of participation in the governance of this country. When a backward class candidate becomes a Collector or a Superintendent of Police, the material benefits accruing from his position are limited to the members of his family only. But the psychological spin off of this phenomenon is tremendous; the entire community of that backward class candidate feels socially elevated. Even when no tangible benefits flow to the community at large, the feeling that now it has its 'own man' in the 'corridors of power' acts as morale booster.

In a democratic set-up every individual and community has a legitimate right and aspiration to participate in ruling this country. Any situation which results in a near-denial of this right to nearly 52 per cent of the country's population needs to be urgently rectified.

Apprehensions regarding drop in the quality of government services owing to large scale induction of SC/ST and OBC candidates against reserved posts may be justified only up to a point. But is it possible to maintain that all candidates selected on merit turn out to be honest, efficient, hard-working and dedicated? At present, top echelons of all the government services are manned predominantly by open competition candidates and if the performance of our bureaucracy is any indication, it has not exactly covered itself with glory. Of course, this does not imply that candidates selected against reserved posts will do better. Chances are that owing to their social and cultural handicaps they may be generally a shade less competent. But, on the other hand, they will have the great advantage of possessing first hand knowledge of the sufferings and problems of the backward sections of society. This is not a small asset for field workers and policy makers even at the highest level.

It is no doubt true that the major benefits of reservation and other welfare measures for other backward classes will be cornered by the more advanced sections of the backward communities. But is not this a universal phenomenon? All reformist remedies have to contend with a slow recovery along the hierarchical gradient; there are no quantum jumps in social reform. Moreover, human nature being what it is, a 'new class' ultimately does emerge even in classless societies. The chief merit of reservation is not that it will introduce egalitarianism amongst OBCs when the rest of the Indian society is seized by all sorts of inequalities. But reservation will certainly erode the hold of higher castes on the services and enable OBCs in general to have a sense of participation in running the affairs of their country.

It is certainly true that reservation for OBCs will cause a lot of heart-burning to others. But should the mere fact of this heart-burning be allowed to operate as a moral veto against social reform. A lot of heart-burning was caused to the British when they left India. It burns the hearts of all whites when the black protest against apartheid in South Africa. When the higher castes constituting less than 20 per cent of the country's population subjected the rest to all manner of social injustice, it must have caused a lot of heart-burning to the lower castes. But now that the lower castes are asking for a modest share of the national cake of power and prestige, a chorus of alarm is being raised on the plea that this will cause heart burning to the ruling elite. Of all the spacious arguments advanced against reservation for backward classes, there is none which beats this one about 'heart-burning' in sheer sophistry.

In fact the Hindu society has always operated a very rigorous scheme of reservation, which was internalised through caste system. Eklivya lost his thumb and Shambhuk his neck for their breach of caste rules of reservation. The present furore against reservations for OBCs is not aimed at the principle itself, but against the new class of beneficiaries, as they are now clamouring for a share of the opportunities which were all along monopolised by the higher castes.

Quantum and Scheme of Reservations

scheduled castes and scheduled tribes constitute 22.5 per cent of the country's population. Accordingly, a pro-rata reservation of 22.5 per cent has been made for them in all services and public sector undertakings under the Central Government. In the States also, reservation for SCs and STs is directly proportional to their population in each State.

As stated in the last Chapter (para 12.22) the population of OBCs, both Hindu and non-Hindu, is around 52 per cent of the total population of India. Accordingly, 52 per cent of all posts under the Central Government should be reserved for them. But this provision may go against the law laid down in a number of Supreme Court judgments wherein it has been held that the total quantum of reservation under Articles 15(4) and 16(4) of the Constitution should be below 50 per cent. In view of this the proposed reservation for OBCs would have to be pegged at a figure which, when added to 22.5 per cent for SCs and STs, remains below 50 per cent. In view of this legal constraint, the Commission is obliged to recommend a reservation of 27 per cent only, even though their population is almost twice this figure.

States which have already introduced reservation for OBCs exceeding 27 per cent will remain unaffected by this recommendation.

With the above general recommendation regarding the quantum of reservation, the Commission proposes the following overall scheme of reservation for OBCs:

1. Candidates belonging to OBCs recruited on the basis of merit in an open competition should not be adjusted against their

reservation quota of 27 per cent.

2. The above reservation should also be made applicable to promotion quota at all levels.
3. Reserved quota remaining unfilled should be carried forward for a period of three years and dereserved thereafter.
4. Relaxation in the upper age limit for direct recruitment should be extended to the candidates of OBCs in the same manner as done in the case of SCs and STs.
5. A roster system for each category of posts should be adopted by the concerned authorities in the same manner as presently done in respect of SC and ST candidates.

The above scheme of reservation *in* its *toto* should also be made applicable to all recruitment to public sector undertakings both under the Central and State Governments, as also to nationalised banks.

All private sector undertakings which have received financial assistance from the government in one form or the other should also be obliged to recruit personnel on the aforesaid basis.

All universities and affiliated colleges should also be covered by the above scheme of reservation.

To give proper effect to these recommendations, it is imperative that adequate statutory provisions are made by the government to amend the existing enactments, rules, procedures, etc. to the extent they are not in consonance with the same.

Educational Concessions

Our educational system is elitist in character, results in a high degree of wastage and is least suited to the requirements of an over-populated and developing country. It is a legacy of the British rule which was severely criticised during the independence struggle, and yet, it has not undergone any structural changes. Though it is least suited to the needs of backward classes, yet, they are forced to run the rat-race with others as no options are available to them. As 'educational reform' was not within the terms of reference of this Commission, we are also forced to trend the beaten track and suggest only the palliative measure within the existing framework.

Various State Governments are giving a number of educational concessions to Other Backward Class students (Chapter IX, paras

9.30-9.33) like exemption of tuition fees, free supply of books and clothes, mid-day meals, special hostel facilities stipends, etc. These concessions are all right as far as they go. But they do not go for enough. What is required is, perhaps, not so much the provision of additional funds as the framing of integrated schemes for creating the proper environment and incentives for serious and purposeful studies.

It is well known that most backward class children are irregular and indifferent students and their drop-out rate is very high.There are two main reasons for this. First, these children are brought up in a climate of extreme social and cultural deprivation and, consequently, a proper motivation for schooling is generally lacking. Secondly, most of these children come from very poor homes and their parents are forced to press them into doing small chores from a very young age.

Upgrading the cultural environment is a very slow process. Transferring these children to an artificially upgraded environment is beyond the present resources of the country. In view of this it is recommended that this problem may be tackled on a limited and selective basis on two fronts.

First, an intensive and time bound programme for adult education should be launched in selected pockets with high concentration of OBC population. This is a basic motivational approach, as only proprob motivated parents will take serious interest in educating their children. Secondly, residential schools should be set up in these areas for backward class students to provide a climate specially conducive to serious studies. All facilities in these schools including board and lodging, will have to be provided free of cost to attract students from poor and backward homes, separate government hostels for OBC students with the above facilities will be another step in the right direction.

A beginning on both these fronts will have to be made on a limited scale and selective basis. But the scope of these activities should be expanded as fast as the resources permit. Adult education programme and residential schools started on a selective basis will operate as growing-points of consciousness for the entire community and their multiplier effect is bound to be substantial. Whereas several States are extended a number of *ad hoc* concessions to backward class students, few serious attempts have been made to integrate these facilities into a comprehensive scheme for a qualitative upgradation of educational environment available to OBC students.

After all, education is the best catalyst of change and educating the backward classes is the surest way to improve their self image and raise their social status. As OBCs cannot afford the high wastage rates or our educational system, it is very important that their education is highly biased in favour of vocational training. After all reservation in services will absorb only a very small percentage of the educated backward classes and the rest should be suitably equipped with vocational skills to enable them to get a return on having invested several years in education.

It is also obvious that even if all the above facilities are given to OBC students, they will not be able to compete on an equal footing with others in securing admission to technical and professional institutions. In view of this it is recommended that seats should be reserved for OBC students in all scientific, technical and professional institutions run by the Central as well as State Governments. This reservation will fall under Article 15(4) of the Constitution and the quantum of reservation should be the same as in the government services, i.e. 27 per cent. Those States which have already reserved more than 27 per cent seats for OBC students will remain unaffected by this recommendation.

While implementing the provision for reservation it should also be ensured that the candidates who are admitted against the reserved quota are enabled to derive full benefit of higher studies. It has been generally noticed that these OBC students coming from an impoverished cultural background, are not able to keep abreast with other students. It is, therefore, very essential that special coaching facilities are arranged for all such students in our technical and professional institutions. The concerned authorities should clearly appreciate that their job is not finished once candidates against reserved quota have been admitted to various institutions. In fact the real task starts only after that Unless adequate follow-up action is taken to give special coaching assistance to these students, not only these young people will feel frustrated and humiliated but the country will also be landed with ill-equipped and sub-standard engineers, doctors and other professionals.

Financial Assistance

Vocational communities following hereditary occupations have suffered heavily as a result of industrialisation. Mechanical production and introduction of synthetic materials has robbed the village potter, oil crusher, black-smith, carpenter, etc., of their traditional means of livelihood and the pauperisation of these classes is a well known phenomenon in the country-side.

It has, therefore, become very necessary that suitable institutional finance and technical assistance is made available to such members of village vocational communities who want to set up small scale industries on their own. Similar assistance should also be provided to those promising OBC candidates who have obtained special vocational training.

Of course, most State Governments have created various financial and technical agencies for the promotion of small and medium scale industries. But it is well known that only the more influential members of the community are able to derive benefits from these agencies. In view of this, it is very essential that separate financial institutions for providing financial and technical assistance are established for the backward classes. Some State Governments like Karnataka and Andhra Pradesh have already set up separate financial corporations etc. for OBCs.

Cooperative Societies of occupational groups will also help a lot. But due care should be taken that all the office-bearers and members of such societies belong to the concerned hereditory occupational groups and outsiders are not allowed to exploit them by infiltrating into such cooperatives.

The share of OBCs in the industrial and business life of the country is negligible and this partly explains their extremely low income levels. As a part of its overall strategy to uplift the backward classes, it is imperative that all State Governments are suitably advised and encouraged to create a separate network of financial and technical institutions to foster business and industrial enterprise among OBCs.

Structural Changes

Reservations in government employment and educational institutions, as also all possible financial assistance will remain mere palliatives unless the problem of backwardness is tackled at its root. Bulk of the small land-holders, tenants, agricultural labour, impoverished village artisans, unskilled workers, etc. belong to scheduled castes, scheduled tribes and other backward classes. 'Apart from social traditions, the dominance by the top peasantry is exercised through recourse to informal bondage which arises mainly through money-lending, leasing out of small bits of land and providing house-sites and dwelling space to poor peasants. As most of the functionaries of government are drawn from the top peasantry, the class and caste linkage between the functionaries of government and the top peasantry remain firm. This also tilts the socio-political balance in favour of the top peasantry and helps it in having its dominance over others.'

The net outcome of the above situation is that notwithstanding their numerical preponderance, backward classes continue to remain in mental and material bondage of the higher castes and rich peasantry. Consequently, despite constituting nearly three-fourths of the country's population, scheduled castes, scheduled tribes and other backward classes have been able to acquire a very limited political clout, even though adult franchise was introduced more than three decades back. Through their literal monopoly of means of production the higher castes are able to manipulate and coeree the backward classes into acting against their own interest. In view of this, until the stranglehold of the existing production relations is broken through radical land reforms, the abject dependence of under privileged classes on the dominant higher castes will continue indefinitely. In fact there is already a sizeable volume of legislation on the statute books to abolish zamindari, place ceilings on land holdings and distribute laned to the landless. But in actual practice its implementation has been halting, half-hearted and superficial. The States like Karnataka, Kerala and West Bengal which have gone about the job more earnestly have not only succeeded in materially helping the Backward classes, but also reaped rich political dividends into the bargain. A radical transformation of the existing production relations is the most important single step that can be taken for the welfare and upliftment of all backward classes. Even if this is not possible in the industrial sector for various reasons, in the agricultural sector a change of this nature is both feasible and overdue. State Governments should therefore, be directed to enact and implement progressive land legislation so as to effect basic structural changes in the existing production relations in the countryside.

At present surplus land is being allotted to SCs and STs. A part of the surplus land becoming available in future as a result of the operation of land ceiling laws etc. should also be allotted to the OBC.

Miscellaneous

(1) Certain sections of some occupational communities like Fishermen, Banjaras, Bansforas, Khatwes etc. still suffer from the stigma of untouchability in some parts of the country. They have been listed as OBCs, by the Commission, but their inclusion in the lists of scheduled castes/scheduled tribes may be considered by the government.
(2) Backward Classes Development Corporations should be set up both at Central and State levels to implement various socio-educational and economic measures for their advancement.
(3) A separate Ministry/Department for OBCs at the Centre and the States should be created to safeguard their interests.
(4) With a view to giving better representation to certain very backward sections of OBCs, like the Gaddis in Himachal Pradesh, Neo-Buddhists in Maharashtra, Fishermen in the Coastal areas, Gujjars in J & K, it is recommended that areas of their concentration may be carved out into separate constituencies.

Central Assistance

At present no central assistance is available to any State Government for implementing any welfare measures for other backward classes. The eighteen states and union territories which have undertaken such measures have to provide funds from their own resources. During the Commission's tours practically every state government pointed out that unless the centre is prepared to liberally. Finance all special schemes for the upliftment of OBCs, it will be beyond the available resources of the states to undertake any worthwhile programme for the benefit of other backward classes. All development programmes specially designed for other backward classes should be financed by the Central Government in the same manner and to the same extent as done in the case of scheduled castes and scheduled tribes.

Regarding the period of operation of the Commission's recommendations, the entire scheme should be reviewed after twenty years. We have advisedly suggested this span of one generation, as the raising of social consciousness is a generational progress. Any review at a shorter interval would be rather arbitrary and will not give a fair indication of the impact of our recommendations on the prevailing status and life-styles of other backward classes.

Index